Heinemann First
ENCYCLOPEDIA

Index

Heinemann Library
Chicago, Illinois

© 1999, 2006 Heinemann Library
a division of Reed Elsevier Inc.
Chicago, Illinois

Customer Service   888–454–2279

Visit our website at www.heinemannlibrary.com

Series Editors: Rebecca and Stephen Vickers, Gianna Williams
Author Team: Rob Alcraft, Catherine Chambers, Sabrina Crewe, Jim Drake, Fred Martin, Angela Royston, Jane Shuter, Roger Thomas, Rebecca Vickers, Stephen Vickers

This revised and expanded edition produced for Heinemann Library by Discovery Books.
Photo research by Katherine Smith and Rachel Tisdale
Designed by Keith Williams, Michelle Lisseter, and Gecko
Illustrations by Joanne Cowne, David Mostyn, Oxford Illustrators, Stefan Chabluk, and Mark Bergin

Originated by Ambassador Litho Limited
Printed in China by WKT Company Limited

10 09 08 07 06
10 9 8 7 6 5 4 3 2

Library of Congress Cataloging-in-Publication Data

Heinemann first encyclopedia.
       p.   cm.
     Summary: A fourteen-volume encyclopedia covering animals, plants, countries, transportation, science, ancient civilizations, US states, US presidents, and world history
     ISBN 1-4034-7120-7 (v. 13 : lib. bdg.)
     1.   Children's encyclopedias and dictionaries.
  I. Heinemann Library (Firm)
  AG5.H45 2005
  031—dc22
2005006176

Contents

THE FACTFILE

A World of Countries........................4

Land and Sea........................6

Where People Live........................7

Hot and Cold: January........................8

Hot and Cold: July........................9

A World of Plants........................10

Plant Classification........................11

Animal Classification........................11

World History up to 1900........................12

Modern World History........................14

U.S. History........................16

The United States........................18

U.S. Land Features........................20

U.S. Government........................22

State Symbols........................23

U.S. Presidents........................26

How a Bill Becomes Law........................29

THE INDEX

How to Use the Index........................30

The Subject List........................31

The Index........................37

A World of Countries

This is a map of the countries in the world. It shows the lines where one country finishes, and the next begins. These lines are called borders.

Some borders between countries follow rivers or mountains. Other borders are straight lines. They can divide people who speak the same language, or live in the same way.

As you look at it remember that the world is really round like an orange. This map is like the earth's skin flattened out. It makes it easier to look at on a page, but does make some countries look bigger than they really are. For instance, Greenland is not really as big as it looks. South America should look a little bigger.

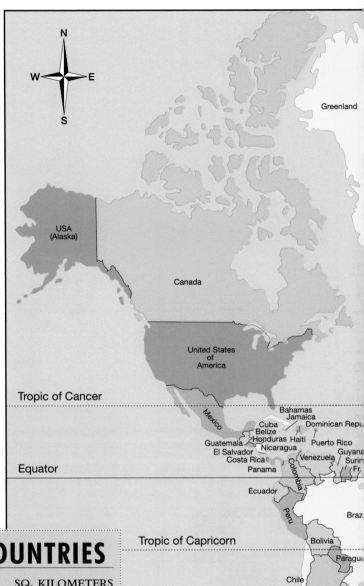

THE TEN BIGGEST COUNTRIES

COUNTRY	SQ. MILES	SQ. KILOMETERS
RUSSIA	6,590,950	17,075,000
CANADA	3,850,790	9,976,140
CHINA	3,704,426	9,596,960
USA	3,617,827	9,372,610
BRAZIL	3,285,620	8,511,970
AUSTRALIA	2,967,124	7,686,850
INDIA	1,269,000	3,287,590
ARGENTINA	1,071,879	2,776,890
KAZAKHSTAN	1,048,877	2,717,300
SUDAN	967,242	2,505,810

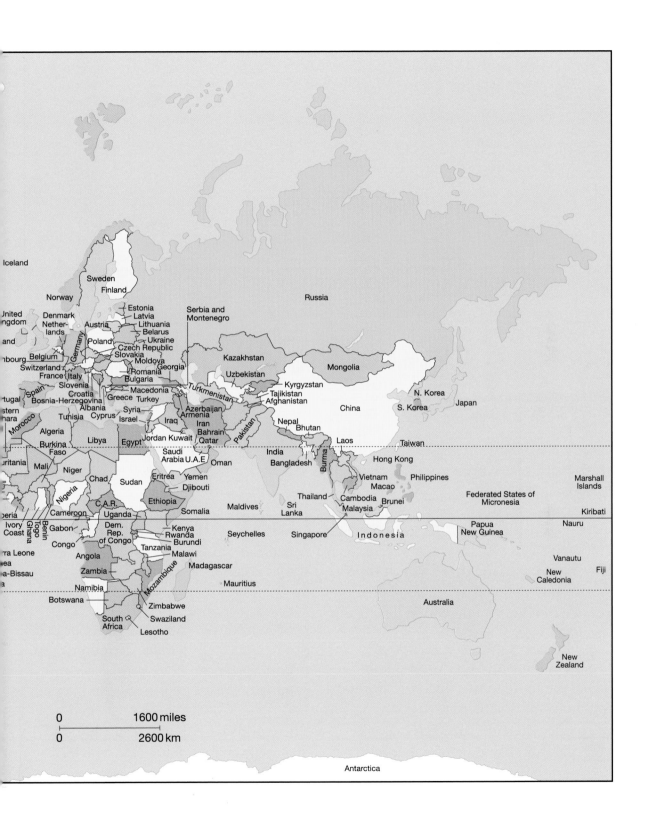

Iceland

Sweden
Finland
Norway

Russia

Estonia
Latvia
Serbia and
Montenegro

United
Kingdom
Denmark
Nether-
lands
Austria
Lithuania
Belarus

and

Germany
Poland
Czech Republic
Ukraine
Slovakia
Moldova
Kazakhstan
Mongolia

bourg
Belgium

Switzerland
Romania
Georgia

France
Italy
Bulgaria

Slovenia
Turkmenistan
Uzbekistan

Spain
Croatia
Macedonia
Kyrgyzstan

Portugal
Bosnia-Herzegovina
Greece
Turkey
Tajikistan
N. Korea

stern
Albania
Syria
Azerbaijan
Afghanistan
China
S. Korea
Japan

hara
Tunisia
Cyprus
Armenia

Morocco
Israel
Iraq
Iran
Nepal
Bhutan

Algeria
Jordan
Kuwait
Bahrain
Qatar
Pakistan
Laos
Taiwan

Burkina
Libya
Egypt
India
Burma

Faso
Saudi
Arabia
U.A.E
Oman
Bangladesh
Hong Kong

uritania
Mali
Niger
Chad
Sudan
Eritrea
Yemen
Vietnam
Macao
Philippines
Marshall
Islands

Nigeria
Djibouti
Thailand
Cambodia
Brunei
Federated States of
Micronesia
Kiribati

C.A.R.
Ethiopia
Somalia
Maldives
Sri
Lanka
Malaysia

eria
Cameroon
Uganda
Nauru

Ivory
Coast
Benin
Togo
Ghana
Gabon
Kenya
Rwanda
Burundi
Seychelles
Singapore
Indonesia
Papua
New Guinea

ra Leone
Congo
Dem.
Rep.
of Congo
Tanzania
Malawi
Vanatu

wea
Angola
Madagascar
New
Caledonia
Fiji

a-Bissau
Zambia
Mozambique
Mauritius

Namibia
Zimbabwe
Australia

Botswana
Swaziland

South
Africa
Lesotho

New
Zealand

```
0            1600 miles
0            2600 km
```

Antarctica

Land and Sea

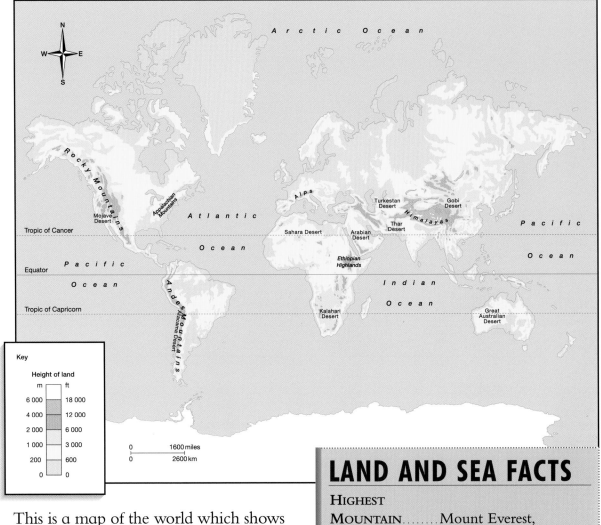

This is a map of the world which shows water and the height of the land. You can see that most of the world's surface is ocean and sea.

Only one-fourth of the world is land. There are mountains, which on this map are shown as shadowed areas. Mountains are made where the land has become crumpled, just like a giant paper bag being crushed into a ball. The highest mountains are in the Himalayas, in Asia.

LAND AND SEA FACTS

HIGHEST
MOUNTAIN........Mount Everest,
　　　　　　　29,028 ft., Himalayas

DEEPEST PLACE
IN THE OCEAN...Mariana Trench in the
　　　　　　　Pacific Ocean, 6.8 miles

LONGEST RIVER.Nile, Africa

BIGGEST DESERT.Sahara, Africa

The world's deserts, where it is hot and dry, are usually in low areas. Much of Australia is desert. Africa has the world's largest desert, called the Sahara.

Where People Live

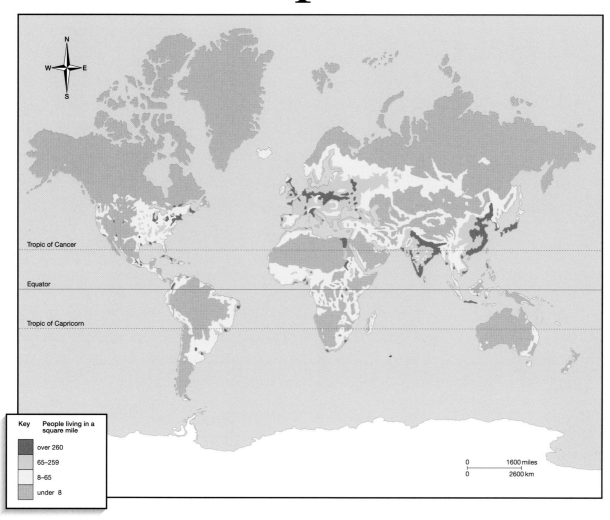

Key — People living in a square mile

- over 260
- 65–259
- 8–65
- under 8

Tropic of Cancer

Equator

Tropic of Capricorn

0 — 1600 miles
0 — 2600 km

This is a map of the world which shows where people live.

Most of the world has few people. These areas are colored pale blue. In some of these places it is too cold to live easily. Some of it is desert, and too hot and dry to grow food. Very few people live in the world's high mountains.

The brown colors show where the greatest number of people live. They live in the lowland areas of the world. Here there is rain, and good land to grow food.

Over half the world's people live in the lowlands of India and East Asia. Europe also has many people. The most crowded places are the big cities.

POPULATION FACTS

LARGEST CITY .... Tokyo in Japan, with over 26 million people

COUNTRY WITH MOST PEOPLE ..... China has almost 1.3 billion people

Hot and Cold: January

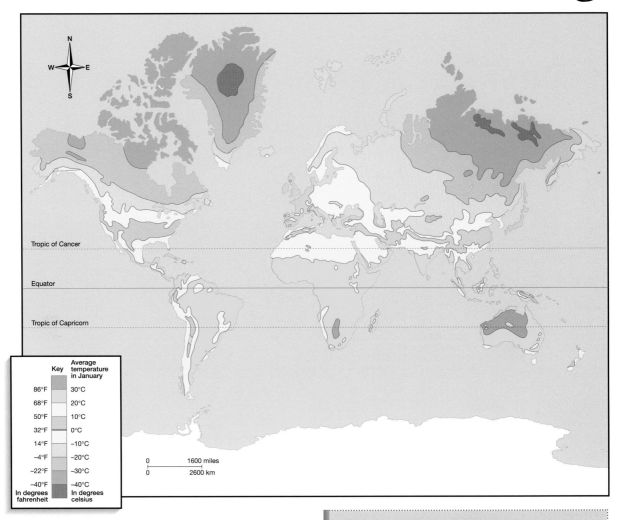

Key	Average temperature in January
86°F	30°C
68°F	20°C
50°F	10°C
32°F	0°C
14°F	-10°C
-4°F	-20°C
-22°F	-30°C
-40°F	-40°C
In degrees fahrenheit	In degrees celsius

Tropic of Cancer

Equator

Tropic of Capricorn

0   1600 miles
0   2600 km

This is a map of the world in January. This is the time of year when the northern half of the world is farthest away from the sun. This means that for these countries the days are short, and it is cold.

In the far north, the sun does not shine at all. It is dark all day, and very, very cold. For northern countries such as Sweden and Canada, it is cold and wintery. On the map these places are colored in pale gray.

WET AND DRY

WETTEST PLACE.. Meghalaya in India is the wettest. It has 467 inches of rain a year.

DRIEST PLACE..... Atacama Desert in Chile. It hasn't rained there for 400 years.

Most of the warm places in this January map are in the south. In places like Australia and South America, it is summer. The weather is hot, and the days are long.

Hot and Cold: July

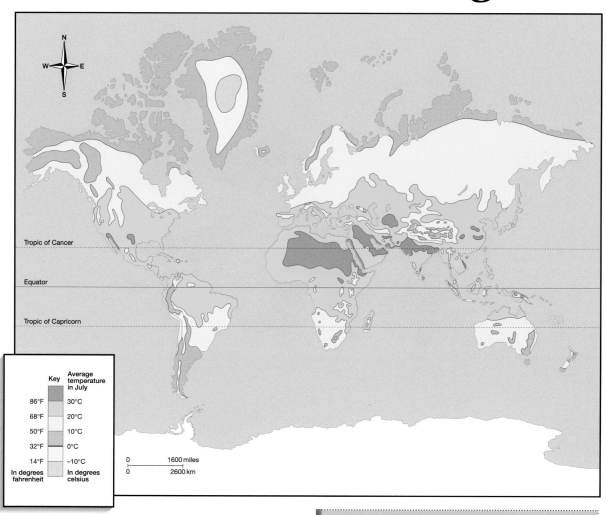

Key

	Average temperature in July
86°F	30°C
68°F	20°C
50°F	10°C
32°F	0°C
14°F	−10°C
In degrees fahrenheit	In degrees celsius

Tropic of Cancer

Equator

Tropic of Capricorn

0   1600 miles
0   2600 km

This is a map of the world in July. This is when northern countries are closest to the sun. In the United States and Canada it is summer. The days become longer, and the weather is warm.

In the far north, the sun never goes down. There is daylight all the time, although there is still snow and ice.

Compare this map to the one on the opposite page. Can you see that there are very few cold places in July?

HOT AND COLD

HOTTEST PLACE .. The hottest temperature that anyone has recorded is 136°F, in Al Azizyah in Libya.

COLDEST PLACE .. The coldest temperature anyone has recorded is −128.6°F at Vostok in Antarctica.

In July the only really cold places are in the far north, and far south. In the very high mountains it is always cold, too.

A World of Plants

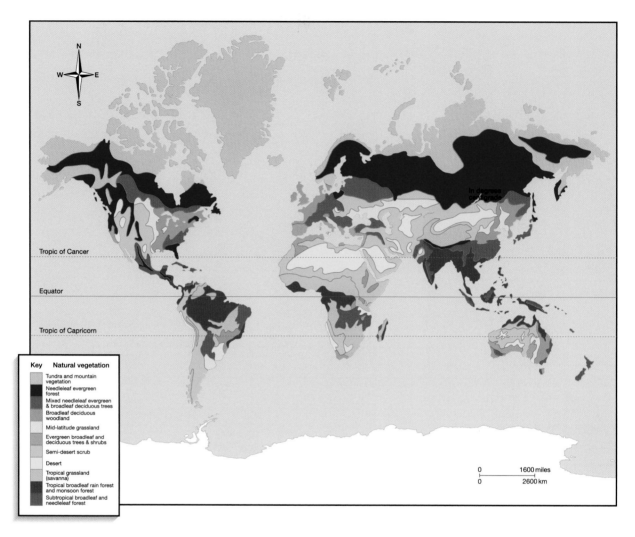

This map shows the kinds of plants that grow around the world. Different plants grow depending on how cold or hot it is, or how wet or dry.

Plants grow best where the weather is always hot and wet. We call these places tropical. On the map they are red. The plants can grow all year. There is hot sun, and lots of rain.

In North America and Europe there is plenty of rain for plants, but it is much cooler. There are seasons. Many plants grow only in summer. In winter they drop their leaves.

In places where it is very dry, or very cold, few plants can grow. These are places like deserts, which are colored yellow on the map.

Plant Classification

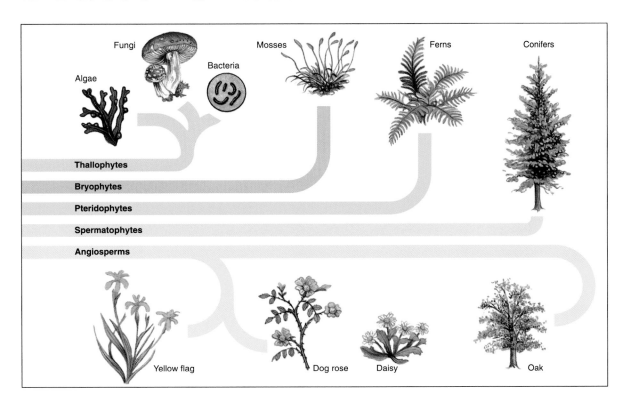

Algae · Fungi · Bacteria · Mosses · Ferns · Conifers

Thallophytes

Bryophytes

Pteridophytes

Spermatophytes

Angiosperms

Yellow flag · Dog rose · Daisy · Oak

Animal Classification

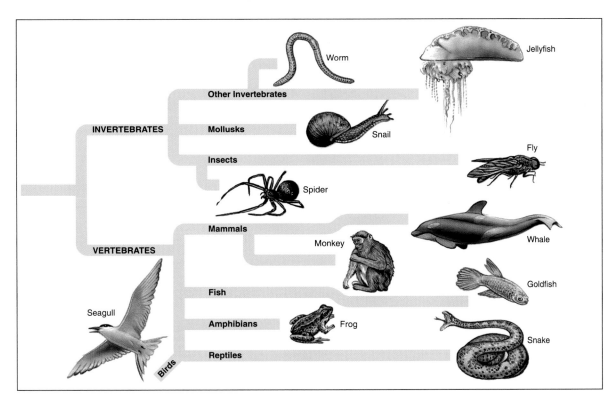

Worm · Jellyfish

Other Invertebrates

INVERTEBRATES

Mollusks · Snail

Insects · Fly

Spider

Mammals · Monkey · Whale

VERTEBRATES

Fish · Goldfish

Seagull

Amphibians · Frog

Birds

Reptiles · Snake

World History up to 1900

These pages shows some of the events during 5000 years of the world's history. Your great-great-grandparents were born in the years on the far right of these pages. On the far left page, no one can be completely sure what happened.

DINOSAURS 150,000,000 YEARS

TO THE MODERN WORLD

3000 BC
World population is about 80 million.

563 BC
The Buddh[a]
born in Ind[ia]

2800 BC
Stonehenge is built.

725 BC
First clock invented in China.

2575 BC
Great Pyramids begun in Egypt.

753 BC
The city of Rome is founded.

2500 BC
Aborigines living in Australia.

776 BC
First Olympic Games held in Greece.

2500 BC
China using bronze tools.

2250 BC
First map is made in Sumeria (now Iraq).

1300 BC
Olmec people build pyramids in Mexico.

2000 BC
Minoan civilization in Crete at its peak.

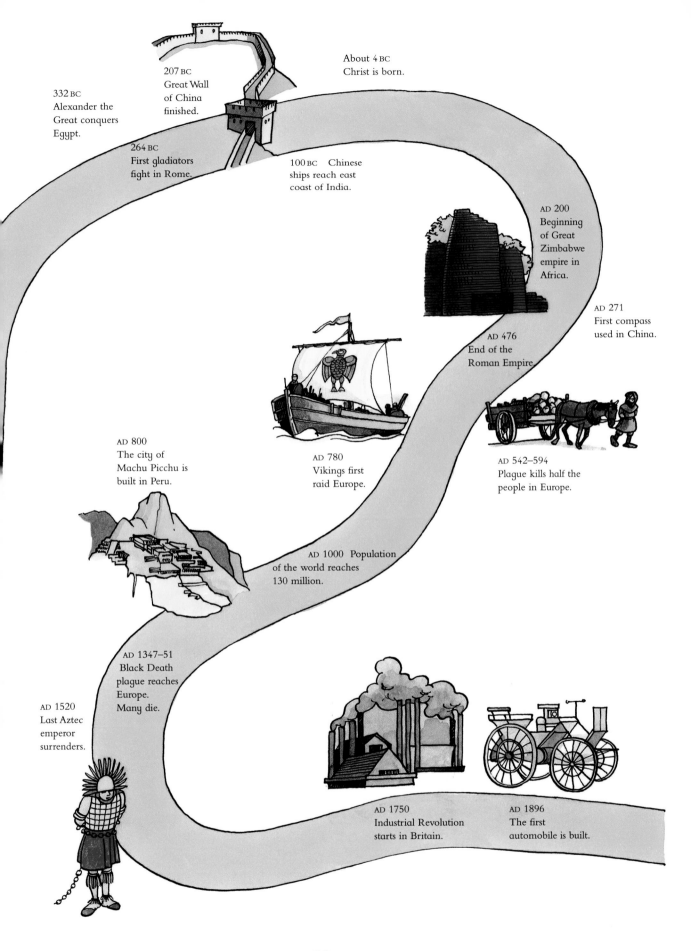

332 BC
Alexander the Great conquers Egypt.

264 BC
First gladiators fight in Rome.

207 BC
Great Wall of China finished.

100 BC   Chinese ships reach east coast of India.

About 4 BC
Christ is born.

AD 200
Beginning of Great Zimbabwe empire in Africa.

AD 271
First compass used in China.

AD 476
End of the Roman Empire.

AD 542–594
Plague kills half the people in Europe.

AD 800
The city of Machu Picchu is built in Peru.

AD 780
Vikings first raid Europe.

AD 1000   Population of the world reaches 130 million.

AD 1347–51
Black Death plague reaches Europe. Many die.

AD 1520
Last Aztec emperor surrenders.

AD 1750
Industrial Revolution starts in Britain.

AD 1896
The first automobile is built.

Modern World History

On these pages are some of the things that have happened since 1900. The year in which you were born is to the far right of these pages. The furthest to the right is where we are now. Do you recognize any of the things that have happened in history?

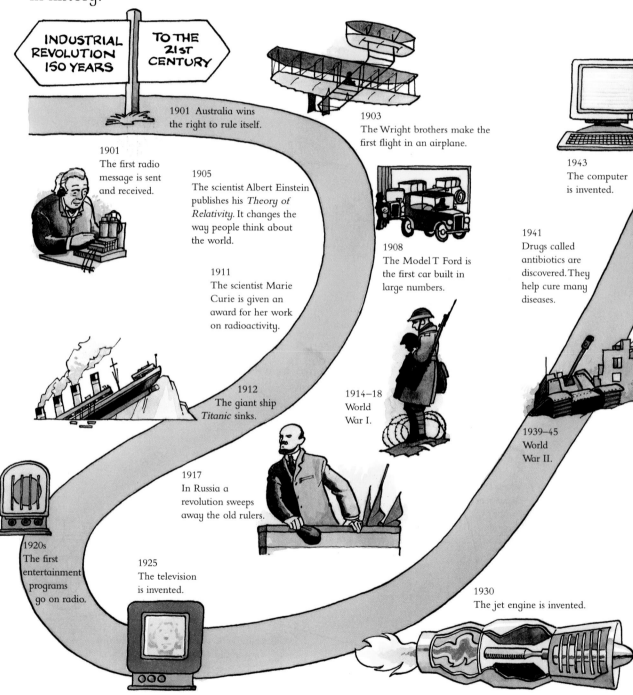

INDUSTRIAL REVOLUTION 150 YEARS

TO THE 21st CENTURY

1901 Australia wins the right to rule itself.

1901 The first radio message is sent and received.

1903 The Wright brothers make the first flight in an airplane.

1905 The scientist Albert Einstein publishes his *Theory of Relativity*. It changes the way people think about the world.

1908 The Model T Ford is the first car built in large numbers.

1911 The scientist Marie Curie is given an award for her work on radioactivity.

1943 The computer is invented.

1941 Drugs called antibiotics are discovered. They help cure many diseases.

1912 The giant ship *Titanic* sinks.

1914–18 World War I.

1939–45 World War II.

1917 In Russia a revolution sweeps away the old rulers.

1920s The first entertainment programs go on radio.

1925 The television is invented.

1930 The jet engine is invented.

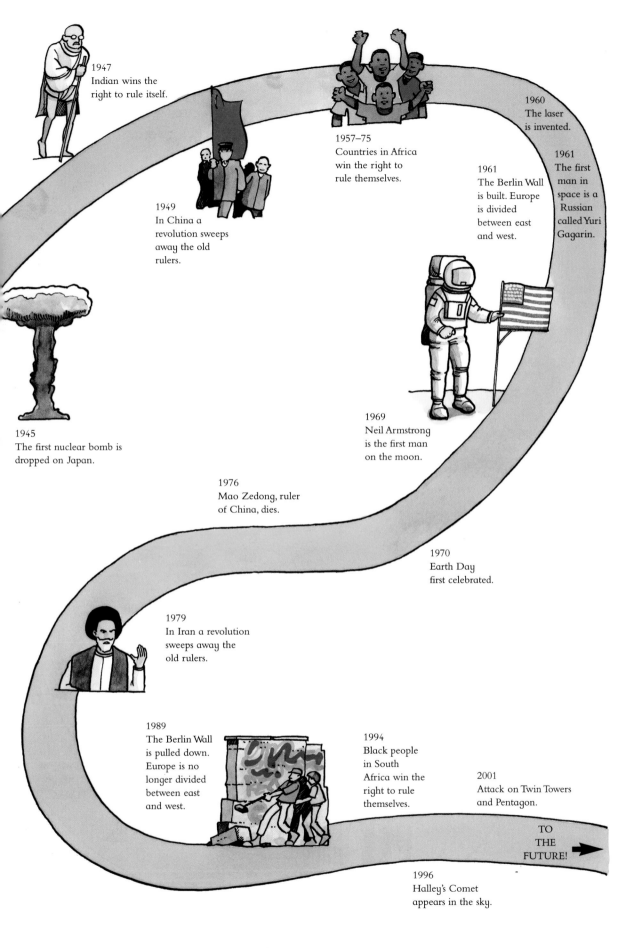

1947
Indian wins the
right to rule itself.

1957–75
Countries in Africa
win the right to
rule themselves.

1960
The laser
is invented.

1949
In China a
revolution sweeps
away the old
rulers.

1961
The Berlin Wall
is built. Europe
is divided
between east
and west.

1961
The first
man in
space is a
Russian
called Yuri
Gagarin.

1945
The first nuclear bomb is
dropped on Japan.

1969
Neil Armstrong
is the first man
on the moon.

1976
Mao Zedong, ruler
of China, dies.

1970
Earth Day
first celebrated.

1979
In Iran a revolution
sweeps away the
old rulers.

1989
The Berlin Wall
is pulled down.
Europe is no
longer divided
between east
and west.

1994
Black people
in South
Africa win the
right to rule
themselves.

2001
Attack on Twin Towers
and Pentagon.

TO
THE
FUTURE!

1996
Halley's Comet
appears in the sky.

U.S. History

These pages show some of the events during almost 600 years of U.S. history. You will have read about many of these things in the Encyclopedia. You might have heard about some of these events at home, on TV, or at school.

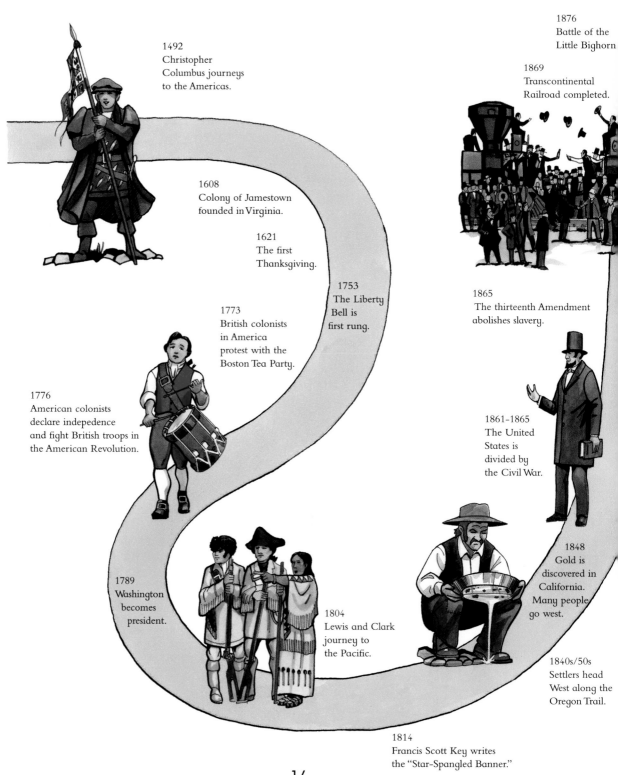

1492
Christopher Columbus journeys to the Americas.

1876
Battle of the Little Bighorn

1869
Transcontinental Railroad completed.

1608
Colony of Jamestown founded in Virginia.

1621
The first Thanksgiving.

1753
The Liberty Bell is first rung.

1773
British colonists in America protest with the Boston Tea Party.

1865
The thirteenth Amendment abolishes slavery.

1776
American colonists declare indepedence and fight British troops in the American Revolution.

1861–1865
The United States is divided by the Civil War.

1789
Washington becomes president.

1804
Lewis and Clark journey to the Pacific.

1848
Gold is discovered in California. Many people go west.

1840s/50s
Settlers head West along the Oregon Trail.

1814
Francis Scott Key writes the "Star-Spangled Banner."

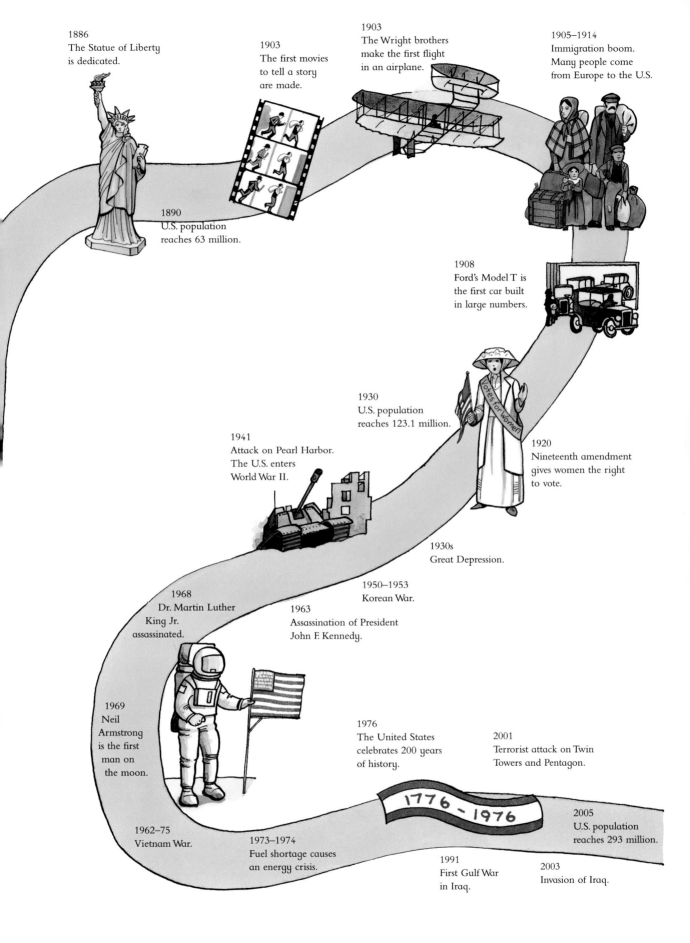

1886
The Statue of Liberty is dedicated.

1903
The first movies to tell a story are made.

1903
The Wright brothers make the first flight in an airplane.

1905–1914
Immigration boom. Many people come from Europe to the U.S.

1890
U.S. population reaches 63 million.

1908
Ford's Model T is the first car built in large numbers.

1930
U.S. population reaches 123.1 million.

1920
Nineteenth amendment gives women the right to vote.

1941
Attack on Pearl Harbor. The U.S. enters World War II.

1930s
Great Depression.

1968
Dr. Martin Luther King Jr. assassinated.

1950–1953
Korean War.

1963
Assassination of President John F. Kennedy.

1969
Neil Armstrong is the first man on the moon.

1976
The United States celebrates 200 years of history.

2001
Terrorist attack on Twin Towers and Pentagon.

1776 – 1976

2005
U.S. population reaches 293 million.

1962–75
Vietnam War.

1973–1974
Fuel shortage causes an energy crisis.

1991
First Gulf War in Iraq.

2003
Invasion of Iraq.

Vofes for Women

The United States

This is a map of the United States. It shows the 50 states and their capitals, as well as important cities. This map also shows the country's capital, Washington, D.C. Each state is colored differently to help you see each one better.

The line between one state and the other is called a border. Often natural features, such as rivers, are the border. Other borders are straight lines. Two of the 50 states are separate from the other 48. These are Alaska and Hawaii.

If you look at a map of the United States like this one, you'll notice how the states are bigger the farther west you go.

U.S. FACTS

LARGEST CITY	New York City, 16.8 million people
LARGEST STATE	Alaska, 571,951 square miles
SMALLEST STATE	Rhode Island, 1,045 square miles
MOST POPULATED STATE	California, 35.5 million people

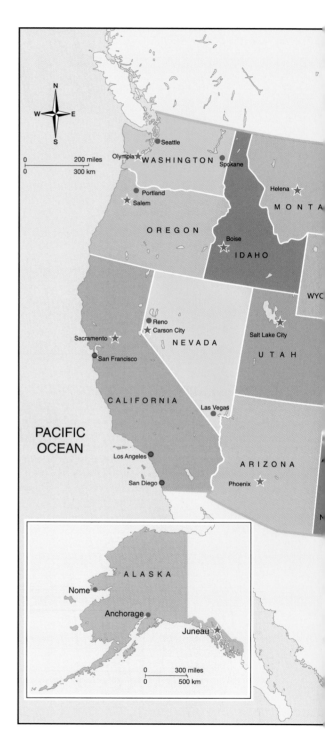

CANADA

National capital
State capitals
Other towns and cities
Country boundaries

MAINE
Augusta
Camden
VERMONT
Burlington
Portland
Montpelier
Concord
NEW HAMPSHIRE
MASSACHUSETTS
Albany
Boston
Buffalo
Providence
NEW YORK
Hartford
RHODE ISLAND
New Haven
CONNECTICUT
New York
NEW JERSEY
PENNSYLVANIA
Trenton
Harrisburg
Philadelphia
Atlantic City
Pittsburgh
Baltimore
Dover
DELAWARE
WASHINGTON D.C.
Annapolis
OHIO
MARYLAND
WEST
Columbus
VIRGINIA
Cincinnati
Charleston
Richmond
Frankfort
VIRGINIA
Norfolk
Louisville
Lexington

NORTH DAKOTA
MINNESOTA
Bismarck
WISCONSIN
Minneapolis
St. Paul
Green Bay
MICHIGAN
Pierre
Madison
Lansing
Detroit
SOUTH DAKOTA
Sioux Falls
Milwaukee
Toledo
Cleveland
Dubuque
Casper
Chicago
NEBRASKA
IOWA
INDIANA
OHIO
Cheyenne
Omaha
Des Moines
ILLINOIS
Lincoln
Indianapolis
Denver
Springfield
Jefferson City
Colorado Springs
Topeka
KANSAS
Kansas City
St. Louis
KENTUCKY
ORADO
Wichita
MISSOURI
Santa Fe
Tulsa
Nashville
Raleigh
NORTH
OKLAHOMA
Charlotte
CAROLINA
Oklahoma City
ARKANSAS
Memphis
TENNESSEE
SOUTH
Little Rock
Huntsville
CAROLINA
Columbia
Dallas
Birmingham
Atlanta
Charleston
MISSISSIPPI
ALABAMA
GEORGIA
Savannah
MEXICO
LOUISIANA
Montgomery
Jackson
TEXAS
Jacksonville
Tallahassee
Austin
Baton Rouge
Houston
New Orleans
Orlando
San Antonio
Tampa
FLORIDA
Miami

ATLANTIC
OCEAN

MEXICO

Honolulu
HAWAII
0   100 miles
0   150 km

–19–

U.S. Land Features

This map of the United States shows what kind of land features there are. It shows all the main rivers, lakes, mountains, plains, and canyons.

The United States has two main mountain ranges crossing it from top to bottom. The Rocky Mountains are in the west, and the Appalachian Mountains are in the east. Between these two mountain ranges are the Great Plains that sit in the center of the country.

LAND AND SEA FACTS

LARGEST LAKE ... Lake Superior, 31,820 square miles

HIGHEST MOUNTAIN .... Mt. McKinley (Mt. Denali), 20,329 feet

LONGEST RIVER .. Mississippi-Missouri-Red Rock river system, 3,860 miles

HOTTEST PLACE . Death Valley, California, 134°F record temperature

LOWEST PLACE .. Death Valley, California, 282 feet below sea level

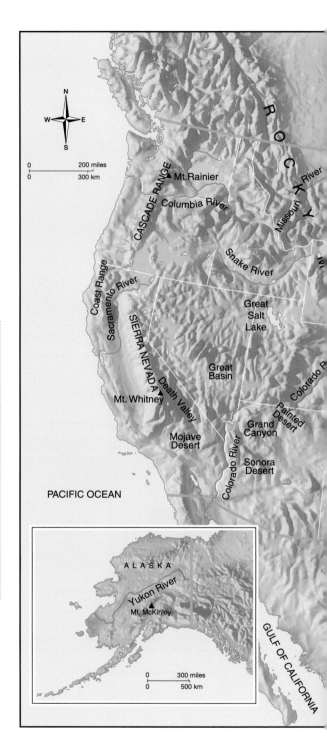

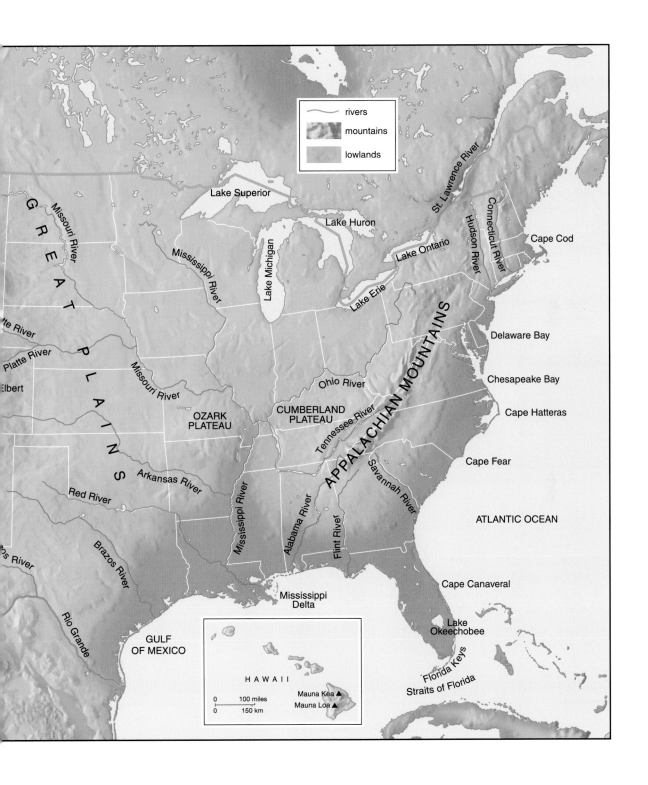

GREAT PLAINS

Missouri River

Platte River

Platte River

Elbert

OZARK PLATEAU

Arkansas River

Red River

Brazos River

os River

Rio Grande

GULF OF MEXICO

Lake Superior

Lake Huron

Lake Michigan

Mississippi River

Lake Ontario

Lake Erie

St. Lawrence River

Connecticut River

Hudson River

Cape Cod

rivers
mountains
lowlands

Delaware Bay

Chesapeake Bay

Cape Hatteras

Cape Fear

ATLANTIC OCEAN

APPALACHIAN MOUNTAINS

Ohio River

CUMBERLAND PLATEAU

Tennessee River

Missouri River

Mississippi River

Alabama River

Flint River

Savannah River

Mississippi Delta

Cape Canaveral

Lake Okeechobee

Florida Keys

Straits of Florida

HAWAII

0   100 miles
0   150 km

Mauna Kea ▲
Mauna Loa ▲

—21—

U.S. Government

The Constitution of the United States divides the U.S. government into three branches. The chart below shows what they are and what each of them does. It also shows how powers are divided between each of the three branches so that no one branch has all the power.

LEGISLATIVE BRANCH

Includes:

Congress (the Senate and the House of Representatives)

The Architect of the Capitol

The Congressional Budget Office

The Government Accountability Office (GAO)

The Government Printing Office

The Library of Congress

The Office of Compliance

The United States Botanic Garden

The most important part of the legislative branch is Congress. Congress makes laws. Both houses of Congress have to approve a new law before it passes. Congress also votes funds. All members of Congress are elected by the people.

EXECUTIVE BRANCH

Includes:

The Executive Office of the president

16 government departments

About 80 independent agencies

The executive branch carries out federal laws. It also creates and enforces regulations based on the laws. The president heads the executive branch. The president can make treaties, can veto or fail to enforce legislation, and can make appointments.

JUDICIAL BRANCH

Includes:

Supreme Court includes eight justices plus the chief justice

Courts of Appeal

District Courts

The judicial branch is the system of law courts. The courts decide if a crime has taken place. The Supreme Court decides whether or not the nation's or a state's laws are Constitutional.

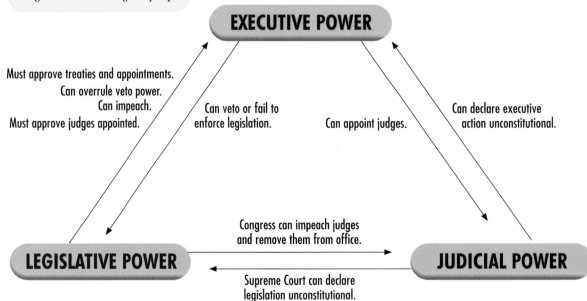

EXECUTIVE POWER

Must approve treaties and appointments.
Can overrule veto power.
Can impeach.
Must approve judges appointed.

Can veto or fail to enforce legislation.

Can appoint judges.

Can declare executive action unconstitutional.

Congress can impeach judges and remove them from office.

Supreme Court can declare legislation unconstitutional.

LEGISLATIVE POWER

JUDICIAL POWER

State Symbols

STATE	FLOWER	BIRD	TREE	MOTTO	SONG	FLAG
Alabama AL	Camellia	Yellow-hammer	Southern longleaf pine	"We dare defend our rights"	"Alabama"	
Alaska AK	Forget-me-not	Willow ptarmigan	Sitka spruce	"North to the future"	"Alaska's Flag"	
Arizona AZ	Blossom of the Saguaro cactus	Cactus wren	Palo verde	"God enriches"	"Arizona"	
Arkansas AR	Apple blossom	Mocking-bird	Pine	"The people rule"	"Arkansas"	
California CA	Golden Poppy	California valley quail	California redwood	"Eureka (meaning, "I have found it")"	"I Love You, California"	
Colorado CO	Rocky Mountain columbine	Lark bunting	Colorado blue spruce	"Nothing without providence"	"Where the Columbines Grow"	
Connecticut CT	Mountain laurel	American robin	White oak	"He who transplanted still sustains"	"Yankee Doodle"	
Delaware DE	Peach blossom	Blue hen chicken	American holly	"Liberty and independence"	"Our Delaware"	
Florida FL	Orange blossom	Mocking-bird	Sabal palmetto palm	"In God we trust"	"The Suwannee River (Old Folks at Home)"	
Georgia GA	Cherokee rose	Brown thrasher	Live oak	"Wisdom, justice, and moderation"	"Georgia on My Mind"	
Hawaii HI	Yellow hibiscus	Nene (Hawaiian goose)	Kukui	"The life of the land is perpetuated in righteousness"	"Hawaii Ponoi"	
Idaho ID	Syringa	Mountain bluebird	Western white pine	"Let it be perpetual"	"Here We Have Idaho"	
Illinois IL	Native violet	Cardinal	White oak	"State sovereignty, national union"	"Illinois"	
Indiana IN	Peony	Cardinal	Tulip poplar	"Crossroads of America"	"On the Banks of the Wabash, Far Away"	
Iowa IA	Wild rose	Eastern goldfinch	Oak	"Our liberties we prize, and our rights we will maintain"	"Song of Iowa"	
Kansas KS	Sunflower	Western meadow-lark	Cotton-wood	"To the stars through difficulties"	"Home on the Range"	

STATE	FLOWER	BIRD	TREE	MOTTO	SONG	FLAG
Kentucky KY	Goldenrod	Cardinal	Tulip poplar	"United we stand, divided we fall"	"My Old Kentucky Home"	
Louisiana LA	Magnolia	Eastern brown pelican	Cypress	"Union, justice, confidence"	"Give Me Louisiana" and "You Are My Sunshine"	
Maine ME	White pine cone and tassel	Chickadee	Eastern white pine	"Dirigo" (meaning "I lead")	"State of Maine Song"	
Maryland MD	Black-eyed Susan	Baltimore oriole	White oak	"Strong deeds, gentle words" or "Manly deeds, womanly words"	"Maryland, My Maryland"	
Massachusetts MA	Mayflower	Chickadee	American elm	"By the sword we seek peace, but peace only under liberty"	"All Hail to Massachusetts"	
Michigan MI	Apple blossom	Robin	White pine	"If you seek a pleasant peninsula, look about you"	"Michigan, My Michigan"	
Minnesota MN	Lady's slipper	Common loon	Red pine	"Star of the north"	"Hail! Minnesota"	
Mississippi MS	Magnolia	Mocking-bird	Magnolia	"By valor and arms"	"Go, Mississippi!"	
Missouri MO	Hawthorn	Bluebird	Flowering dogwood	"The welfare of the people shall be the supreme law"	"Missouri Waltz"	
Montana MT	Bitterroot	Western meadow-lark	Ponderosa pine	"Gold and silver"	"Montana"	
Nebraska NE	Goldenrod	Western meadow-lark	Cotton-wood	"Equality before the law"	"Beautiful Nebraska"	
Nevada NV	Sagebrush	Mountain bluebird	Single-leaf piñon, Bristlecone pine	"All for our country"	"Home Means Nevada"	
New Hampshire NH	Purple lilac	Purple finch	White birch	"Live free or die"	"Old New Hampshire"	
New Jersey NJ	Purple violet	Eastern goldfinch	Red oak	"Liberty and prosperity"	–	
New Mexico NM	Yucca	Road-runner	Piñon	"It grows as it goes"	"O Fair New Mexico"	
New York NY	Rose	Bluebird	Sugar maple	"Ever upward"	"I Love New York"	
North Carolina NC	Dogwood	Cardinal	Pine	"To be rather than to seem"	"The Old North State"	

STATE	FLOWER	BIRD	TREE	MOTTO	SONG	FLAG
North Dakota ND	Wild prairie rose	Western meadowlark	American elm	"Liberty and union, now and forever, one and inseparable"	"North Dakota Hymn"	
Ohio OH	Scarlet carnation	Cardinal	Buckeye	"With God all things are possible"	"Beautiful Ohio"	
Oklahoma OK	Mistletoe	Scissor-tailed flycatcher	Redbud	"Labor conquers all things"	"Oklahoma!"	
Oregon OR	Oregon grape	Western meadowlark	Douglas fir	"She flies with her own wings"	"Oregon, My Oregon"	
Pennsylvania PA	Mountain laurel	Ruffed grouse	Hemlock	"Virtue, liberty, and independence"	"Pennsylvania"	
Rhode Island RI	Common blue violet	Rhode Island red hen	Red maple	"Hope"	"Rhode Island"	
South Carolina SC	Carolina (yellow) jessamine	Carolina wren	Palmetto	"While I breathe, I hope" and "Ready in soul and resource"	"Carolina"	
South Dakota SD	Pasqueflower	Ring-necked pheasant	Black Hills spruce	"Under God, the people rule"	"Hail, South Dakota"	
Tennessee TN	Iris	Mockingbird	Tulip poplar	"Agriculture and commerce"	"My Homeland, Tennessee" (plus 4 others)	
Texas TX	Bluebonnet	Mockingbird	Pecan	"Friendship"	"Texas, Our Texas"	
Utah UT	Sego lily	Seagull	Blue spruce	"Industry"	"Utah, We Love Thee"	
Vermont VT	Red clover	Hermit thrush	Sugar maple	"Freedom and Unity"	"These Green Mountains"	
Virginia VA	Dogwood	Cardinal	Dogwood	"Thus always to tyrants"	"Carry Me Back to Old Virginia"	
Washington WA	Coast rhododendron	Willow goldfinch	Western hemlock	"Al-ki" (meaning, "By and by")	"Washington, My Home"	
West Virginia WV	Rhododendron	Cardinal	Sugar maple	"Mountaineers are always free"	"This is My West Virginia" (plus 2 others)	
Wisconsin WI	Wood violet	Robin	Sugar maple	"Forward"	"On, Wisconsin!"	
Wyoming WY	Indian paintbrush	Western meadowlark	Cottonwood	"Equal rights"	"Wyoming"	

For more information on each state, see individual entries in the encyclopedia.

U.S. Presidents

NAME (DATES)	DATES IN OFFICE	PARTY	VICE PRESIDENT(S)	FIRST LADY
1. George Washington (1732–1799)	1789–1797	Federalist	John Adams	Martha Dandridge Custis Washington
2. John Adams (1735–1826)	1797–1801	Federalist	Thomas Jefferson	Abigail Smith Adams
3. Thomas Jefferson (1743–1826)	1801–1809	Democratic Republican	Aaron Burr George Clinton	–
4. James Madison (1751–1836)	1809–1817	Democratic Republican	George Clinton Elbridge Gerry	Dolley Payne Todd Madison
5. James Monroe (1758–1831)	1817–1825	Democratic Republican	Daniel D. Tompkins	Elizabeth Kortright Monroe
6. John Quincy Adams (1767–1848)	1825–1829	Democratic Republican	John C. Calhoun	Louisa Johnson Adams
7. Andrew Jackson (1767–1845)	1829–1837	Democrat	John C. Calhoun Martin Van Buren	Rachel Robards Jackson
8. Martin Van Buren (1782–1862)	1837–1841	Democrat	Richard M. Johnson	widower
9. William Harrison (1773–1841)	1841	Whig	John Tyler	Anna Symmes Harrison
10. John Tyler (1790–1862)	1841–1845	Whig	–	Letitia Christian Tyler Julia Gardiner Tyler
11. James Knox Polk (1795–1849)	1845–1849	Democrat	George M. Dallas	Sarah Childress Polk
12. Zachary Taylor (1784–1850)	1849–1850	Whig	Millard Fillmore	Margaret Mackall Smith Taylor
13. Millard Fillmore (1800–1874)	1850–1853	Whig	–	Abigail Powers Fillmore
14. Franklin Pierce (1804–1869)	1853–1857	Democrat	William R.D. King	Jane Means Appleton Pierce
15. James Buchanan (1791–1868)	1857–1861	Democrat	John C. Breckinridge	–
16. Abraham Lincoln (1809–1865)	1861–1865	Republican	Hannibal Hamlin Andrew Johnson	Mary Todd Lincoln

Name (Dates)	Dates in office	Party	Vice president(s)	First lady
17. Andrew Johnson (1808–1875)	1865–1869	Democrat	–	Eliza McCardle Johnson
18. Ulysses S. Grant (1822–1885)	1869–1877	Republican	Schuyler Colfax Henry Wilson	Julia Dent Grant
19. Rutherford B. Hayes (1822–1893)	1877–1881	Republican	William A. Wheeler	Lucy Webb Hayes
20. James Garfield (1831–1881)	1881–1881	Republican	Chester A. Arthur	Lucretia Rudolph Garfield
21. Chester A. Arthur (1830–1886)	1881–1885	Republican	–	Ellen Herndon Arthur
22. Grover Cleveland (1837–1908)	1885–1889	Democrat	Thomas A. Hendricks	Frances Folsom Cleveland
23. Benjamin Harrison (1833–1901)	1889–1893	Republican	Levi P. Morton	Caroline Lavinia Scott Harrison
24. Grover Cleveland (1837–1908)	1893–1897	Democrat	Adlai E. Stevenson	Frances Folsom Cleveland
25. William McKinley (1843–1901)	1897–1901	Republican	Garret A. Hobart Theodore Roosevelt	Ida Saxton McKinley
26. Theodore Roosevelt (1858–1919)	1901–1909	Republican	Charles W. Fairbanks	Edith Kermit Carow Roosevelt
27. William H. Taft (1857–1930)	1909–1913	Republican	James S. Sherman	Helen Herron Taft
28. Woodrow Wilson (1856–1924)	1913–1921	Democrat	Thomas R. Marshall	Ellen Axson Wilson Edith Galt Wilson
29. Warren G. Harding (1865–1923)	1921–1923	Republican	Calvin Coolidge	Florence Kling De Wolfe Harding
30. Calvin Coolidge (1872–1933)	1923–1929	Republican	Charles G. Dawes	Grace Anna Goodhue Coolidge
31. Herbert Hoover (1874–1964)	1929–1933	Republican	Charles Curtis	Lou Henry Hoover
32. Franklin D. Roosevelt (1882–1945)	1933–1945	Democrat	John N. Garner Henry A. Wallace Harry S Truman	Eleanor Roosevelt Roosevelt

Name (Dates)	Dates in Office	Party	Vice president(s)	First lady
33. Harry S Truman (1884–1972)	1945–1953	Democrat	Alben W. Barkley	Bess Wallace Truman
34. Dwight Eisenhower (1890–1969)	1953–1961	Republican	Richard M. Nixon	Mamie Doud Eisenhower
35. John F. Kennedy (1917–1963)	1961–1963	Democrat	Lyndon B. Johnson	Jacqueline Bouvier Kennedy
36. Lyndon B. Johnson (1908–1973)	1963–1969	Democrat	Hubert H. Humphrey	Claudia "Lady Bird" Alta Taylor Johnson
37. Richard Nixon (1913–1994)	1969–1974	Republican	Spiro T. Agnew Gerald R. Ford	Thelma Catherine "Pat" Ryan Nixon
38. Gerald Ford (1913–)	1974–1977	Republican	Nelson Rockefeller	Elizabeth "Betty" Bloomer Ford
39. Jimmy Carter (1924–)	1977–1981	Democrat	Walter Mondale	Rosalynn Smith Carter
40. Ronald Reagan (1911–2004)	1981–1989	Republican	George H.W. Bush	Nancy Davis Reagan
41. George H.W. Bush (1924–)	1989–1993	Republican	J. Danforth Quayle	Barbara Pierce Bush
42. Bill Clinton (1946–)	1993–2001	Democrat	Albert Gore	Hillary Rodham Clinton
43. George W. Bush (1946–)	2001–	Republican	Richard B. Cheney	Laura Welch Bush

How a Bill Becomes Law

When politicians want to pass a new law, they first have to introduce a bill. This chart shows the different steps a bill has to go through before it can become a law. A bill can start either in the House or the Senate. This chart shows a bill that starts in the House.

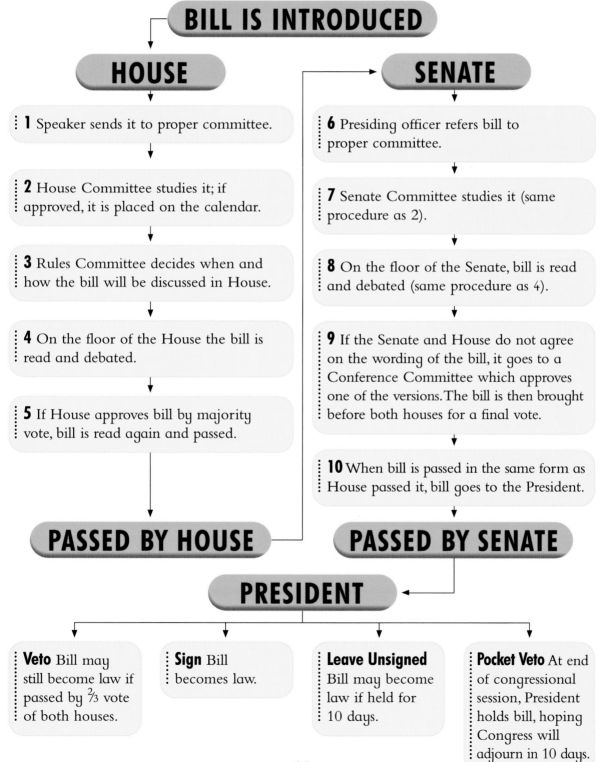

BILL IS INTRODUCED

HOUSE

1 Speaker sends it to proper committee.

2 House Committee studies it; if approved, it is placed on the calendar.

3 Rules Committee decides when and how the bill will be discussed in House.

4 On the floor of the House the bill is read and debated.

5 If House approves bill by majority vote, bill is read again and passed.

SENATE

6 Presiding officer refers bill to proper committee.

7 Senate Committee studies it (same procedure as 2).

8 On the floor of the Senate, bill is read and debated (same procedure as 4).

9 If the Senate and House do not agree on the wording of the bill, it goes to a Conference Committee which approves one of the versions. The bill is then brought before both houses for a final vote.

10 When bill is passed in the same form as House passed it, bill goes to the President.

PASSED BY HOUSE

PASSED BY SENATE

PRESIDENT

Veto Bill may still become law if passed by ⅔ vote of both houses.

Sign Bill becomes law.

Leave Unsigned Bill may become law if held for 10 days.

Pocket Veto At end of congressional session, President holds bill, hoping Congress will adjourn in 10 days.

How to Use the Index

The Subject List (pages 31–36)
The Subject List groups together all entry words in the encyclopedia on a particular subject. For example, under the subject heading DINOSAURS, you will find a list of all the different dinosaur entries in alphabetical order in the whole encyclopedia. The ANIMALS subject list is also divided into types of animals, such as mammals, birds, and fish. The COUNTRIES entries are listed under the continent each country is found in. The main subject headings are in Dewey Decimal order, like books are arranged in most libraries.

The Index (pages 37–48)
The Index lists all the entry words in the encyclopedia and also some other important words. It tells the encyclopedia volume and page number of where the information can be found. Some of the indexed words have *see also* references. These tell you other words to look under in the index to find more information.

Remember: the volume number is followed by a colon (:) and then by the page number.

Find the letter the word you are looking for starts with.

see references tell you where to look to find information.

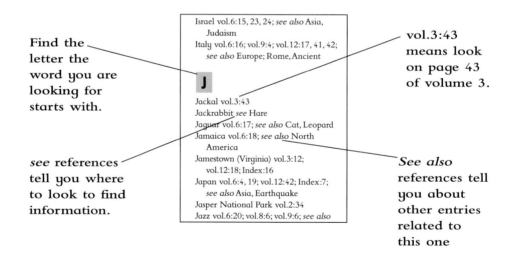

Israel vol.6:15, 23, 24; *see also* Asia, Judaism
Italy vol.6:16; vol.9:4; vol.12:17, 41, 42; *see also* Europe; Rome, Ancient

J

Jackal vol.3:43
Jackrabbit *see* Hare
Jaguar vol.6:17; *see also* Cat, Leopard
Jamaica vol.6:18; *see also* North America
Jamestown (Virginia) vol.3:12; vol.12:18; Index:16
Japan vol.6:4, 19; vol.12:42; Index:7; *see also* Asia, Earthquake
Jasper National Park vol.2:34
Jazz vol.6:20; vol.8:6; vol.9:6; *see also*

vol.3:43 means look on page 43 of volume 3.

See also references tell you about other entries related to this one

The Subject List

The main subject headings are in Dewey Decimal order, like books in libraries.

WORLD RELIGIONS 200

Buddhism
Christianity
Hinduism
Islam
Judaism
Sikhism

TRANSPORTATION 300

Airplane
Balloon
Barge
Bicycle
Bus
Canoe
Car
Helicopter
Hovercraft
Motorcycle
Railroad
Road
Ship
Spacecraft
Submarine
Train
Truck
Waterway

GOVERNMENT AND SOCIAL SCIENCES 300

Anthony, Susan B.
Constitution
Executive Branch
Government
Holiday
Independence
 Day
Judicial Branch
King, Martin
 Luther, Jr.
Legislative Branch
Slavery
Pledge of
 Allegiance
Washington, D.C.

PLANTS 500

Cactus
Fern
Flower
Forest
Fungus
Leaf
Moss
Root
Seed
Stem
Tree
Wood

ANIMALS 500

Amphibians
Frog
Toad

Arachnids
Scorpion
Spider

Birds
Chicken
Crane
Duck
Eagle
Emu
Flamingo
Goose
Gull
Hawk
Hummingbird
Kiwi
Ostrich
Owl
Parrot
Penguin
Pigeon
Seabird
Swan
Vulture
Woodpecker

Crustaceans
Crab
Woodlouse

Fish/Sea Animals
Coral
Eel
Fish, Tropical
Jellyfish
Sea Anemone
Sea Horse
Sea Urchin
Ray
Shark
Starfish

Insects

Ant	Cockroach	Fly	Moth
Bee	Dragonfly	Grasshopper	Praying Mantis
Beetle	Earwig	Ladybug	Termite
Butterfly	Firefly	Lice	Wasp
Caterpillar	Flea	Mosquito	

Mammals

Aardvark	Coyote	Koala	Raccoon
Anteater	Deer	Leopard	Rat
Antelope	Dog	Lion	Rhinoceros
Ape	Dolphin	Marsupial	Sea Lion
Badger	Elephant	Monkey	Seal
Bat	Fox	Moose	Sheep
Bear	Giraffe	Mouse	Skunk
Beaver	Goat	Opossum	Squirrel
Bison	Hare	Otter	Tiger
Buffalo	Hedgehog	Panda	Whale
Camel	Hippopotamus	Pig	Wolf
Cat	Horse	Platypus	Wolverine
Cattle	Jaguar	Porcupine	Zebra
Cheetah	Kangaroo	Rabbit	

Mollusks

Octopus	Snail
Slug	Squid

Reptiles

Alligator	Snake
Crocodile	Tortoise
Lizard	Turtle

Nocturnal animals

Aardvark	Hedgehog
Badger	Hippopotamus
Bat	Kiwi
Cat	Koala
Centipede	Moth
Cockroach	Opossum
Coyote	Owl
Earwig	Rabbit
Firefly	Raccoon
Fox	Slug
Frog	Toad
Hare	

DINOSAURS 500

Brachiosaurus
Pterosaur
Stegosaurus
Triceratops
Tyrannosaurus

WEATHER 500

Air
Climate
Flood
Hurricane
Lightning
Rainbow
Season
Tornado
Water Cycle

SCIENCE AND TECHNOLOGY 500 AND 600

Air
Armstrong, Neil
Bacteria
Bar Code
Blood
Calendar
Camera
Color
Comet
Communication
Computer
Day and Night
Drug
Ear
Edison, Thomas
Egg
Electricity
Endangered
   Species
Energy
Engine
Eye
Food chain
Fuel
Heart
Heat
Hibernation
Human Body
Internet
Laser
Life Cycle
Light
Lung
Machines, Simple
Magnet
Matter
Measurement
Metal
Metamorphosis
Meteor
Migration
Moon
Nutrition
Oxygen
Photosynthesis
Planet
Plastic
Pollution
Radio
Robot
Skeleton
Smell
Solar System
Sound
Space
   Exploration
Star
Sun
Taste
Telephone
Television
Time
Tooth
Touch
Virus
Wright Brothers

THE ARTS 700

Art
Architecture   Painting
Sculpture

Literature
Fable   Myth
Fairy Tale   Poetry
Language   Story
Legend

Music
Classical Music   Percussion
Folk Music   Instrument
Jazz   Pop Music
Musical   Stringed
   Instrument   Instrument
Orchestra   Wind Instrument

Performing Arts
Ballet   Opera
Dance   Puppetry
Drama   Theater

GEOGRAPHY 900

Aborigines   Island
Africa   Lake
Antarctica   Map
Arctic   Mining
Asia   Mountain
Australia   North America
   and Oceania   Ocean
Bay   Peninsula
Coast   Port
Continent   Rain Forest
Crop   River
Delta   Rock
Desert   Season
Earth   South America
Earthquake   Tundra
Europe   Valley
Farming   Volcano
Home   Water

COUNTRIES 900

Africa
Algeria   Madagascar
Botswana   Morocco
Chad   Nigeria
Democratic   Rwanda
   Republic   Somalia
   of Congo   South Africa
Egypt   Sudan
Ethiopia   Tunisia
Ghana   Uganda
Kenya   Zambia
Libya   Zimbabwe

Asia

Afghanistan	Iraq	Nepal	South Korea
Bangladesh	Israel	North Korea	Sri Lanka
Cambodia	Japan	Pakistan	Syria
China	Jordan	Philippines	Taiwan
India	Kuwait	Russia	Thailand
Indonesia	Lebanon	Saudi Arabia	Turkey
Iran	Malaysia	Singapore	Vietnam

Australia and Oceania

Australia	New Zealand	Papua New Guinea

Europe

Albania	Finland	Northern Ireland	Slovenia
Austria	France	Norway	Spain
Belgium	Germany	Poland	Sweden
Bosnia-Herzegovina	Greece	Portugal	Switzerland
Bulgaria	Hungary	Romania	Turkey
Croatia	Iceland	Russia	Ukraine
Czech Republic	Ireland	Scotland	United Kingdom
Denmark	Italy	Serbia and Montenegro	Wales
England	Luxembourg	Slovakia	
	Netherlands		

North America

Bahamas	Cuba	Haiti	Panama
Barbados	Dominican Republic	Honduras	Puerto Rico
Belize		Jamaica	United States of America
Canada	El Salvador	Mexico	
Costa Rica	Guatemala	Nicaragua	

South America

Argentina	Chile	Peru	Venezuela
Bolivia	Colombia	Trinidad and Tobago	
Brazil	Ecuador		

U.S. STATES 900

Alabama	Indiana	Nebraska	South Carolina
Alaska	Iowa	Nevada	South Dakota
Arizona	Kansas	New Hampshire	Tennessee
Arkansas	Kentucky	New Jersey	Texas
California	Louisiana	New Mexico	Utah
Colorado	Maine	New York	Vermont
Connecticut	Maryland	North Carolina	Virginia
Delaware	Massachusetts	North Dakota	Washington
Florida	Michigan	Ohio	Washington, D.C.
Georgia	Minnesota	Oklahoma	West Virginia
Hawaii	Mississippi	Oregon	Wisconsin
Idaho	Missouri	Pennsylvania	Wyoming
Illinois	Montana	Rhode Island	

HISTORY 900

Alphabet	Columbus, Christopher	Industrial Revolution	Rome, Ancient
American Flag	Declaration of Independence	Iron Age	Sacagawea
American Revolution	Egypt, Ancient	Knight	Sitting Bull
Aztecs	Flag	Lewis and Clark	Star-Spangled Banner
Bald Eagle	Fossil	Liberty Bell	Statue of Liberty
Bronze Age	Franklin, Benjamin	Maya	Stone Age
Castle	Greece, Ancient	Middle Ages	Tubman, Harriet
Cathedral	Hieroglyphics	Money	Vikings
China, Ancient	Incas	Native Americans	World War I
Civil War		Olympic Games	World War II
Colonial America		Pyramid	

U.S. PRESIDENTS 900

Adams, John	Roosevelt, Franklin D.
Bush, George W.	
Clinton, Bill	Roosevelt, Theodore
Jefferson, Thomas	
Kennedy, John F.	Washington, George
Lincoln, Abraham	Wilson, Woodrow

The Index

Remember, the volume number is followed by a colon (:), and then by the page number.

A

Aardvark vol.1:4; *see also* Anteater, Mammal

Aardwolf vol.3:34

Abacus vol.8:27

Aborigines vol.1:5; vol.8:7, 8; vol.12:34; Index:12; *see also* Australia, Australia and Oceania

Abuja vol.8:20

Acropolis vol.5:17

Adams, John vol.1:6; vol.2:26; *see also* Bush, George W.; Declaration of Independence; Jefferson, Thomas

Adams, John Quincy vol.1:6; vol.2:26

Addiction vol.3:48

Aesop vol.4:28

Afghanistan vol.1:7; vol.2:26; *see also* Asia

Africa vol.1:8; Index:15; *see also* Continent, Desert

African Americans vol.1:11; vol.6:20, 25, 28, 31; vol.10:42

AIDS vol.12:19

Air vol.1:9; vol.7:12; vol.8:41; vol.10:33; vol.11:36; vol.12:30; *see also* Oxygen, Pollution

Airplane vol.1:10; vol.4:22; vol.8:22; vol.10:39; vol.11:40; vol.12:23, 44; *see also* Helicopter, Transportation, Wright Brothers

Airship vol.1:44

Alabama vol.1:11; vol.6:31; *see also* United States of America

Alaska vol.1:12; vol.6:14; vol.9:18; Index:18; *see also* United States of America

Albania vol.1:13; *see also* Europe

Aldrin, Buzz vol.1:32

Alexander the Great Index:13

Algeria vol.1:14; *see also* Africa, Desert

Alligator vol.1:15; vol.4:40; vol.7:11; vol.9:37; *see also* Crocodile, Reptile

Alloy vol.7:27

Alpaca vol.9:7

Alphabet vol.1:16; vol.2:17; vol.3:38; vol.4:36; vol.5:29; *see also* Hieroglyphics, Language

Alps vol.4:25

Aluminum vol.7:16, 27

Amazon rain forest vol.2:20; vol.4:45; vol.9:33

Amazon River vol.2:16, 20; vol.9:33, 40; vol.10:41

American Falls vol.8:17

American Flag vol.1:17; vol.9:16; vol.11:9; *see also* Flag, Star-Spangled Banner

American Revolution vol.1:6, 18; vol.3:12, 20, 35; vol.5:4, 45; vol.6:21; vol.7:23; vol.11:10; vol.12:18, 25; Index:16; *see also* Colonial America; Declaration of Independence; Washington, George

Amish people vol.9:5

Amphibian vol.1: 19; vol.4:13; vol.5:5; vol.7:4, 28; vol.12:15; *see also* Frog, Metamorphosis, Toad

Amundsen, Roald vol.1:22

Anacostia River vol.12:24

Ancestral Puebloan people vol.3:14

Anchorage (Alaska) vol.1:12

Andersen, Hans Christian vol.3:40; vol.4:29

Anderson, Gerry vol.9:27

Andes Mountains vol.1:29; vol.2:16; vol.3:11; vol.4:10, 43; vol.9:7; vol.10:41; vol.12:13

Animal vol.1:20; vol.3:34; vol.4:44; vol.10:27, 33; vol.11:38; vol.12:15, 27; Index:11; *see also* Invertebrate, Vertebrate

Ant vol.1:21; *see also* Aardvark, Anteater, Insect

Antarctica vol.1:22; vol.8:29; Index:9; *see also* Continent

Anteater vol.1:23; *see also* Aardvark, Mammal

Antelope vol.1: 24; vol.7:8; *see also* Mammal

Anthem vol.11:9

Anthony, Susan B. vol.1:25

Antibiotic Index:14

Apache people vol.1:30

Ape vol.1:26; vol.7:40; *see also* Mammal, Monkey

Aphid vol.4:44

Apollo 11 vol.1:32; vol.4:40; vol.7:42; vol.10:45, 46

Appalachian Mountains vol.4:43; vol.7:22; vol.9:5; vol.12:31; Index:20

Appleseed, Johnny vol.6:42

Aquarium vol.4:35

Arabia vol.9:4

Arabic vol.1:16

Arapaho people vol.7:41; vol.10:26

Araucan people vol.2:46

Arawak Indians vol.6:18

Architecture vol.1:27; vol.2:40; vol.10:47; *see also* Art, Castle, Cathedral, Home

Arctic vol.1:28; vol.2:6; vol.8:29; vol.10:4; vol.11:46; *see also* Tundra

Ardennes vol.2:10

Argentina vol.1:29; Index:4; *see also* South America

Arizona vol.1:30; vol.2:28; vol.7:29, 34; *see also* United States of America

Arkansas vol.1:31; vol.3:8; *see also* United States of America

Armadillo vol.10:41

Armstrong, Louis vol.6:20

Armstrong, Neil vol.1:32; vol.7:42; *see also* Moon, Space Exploration

Art vol.1:5, 33; vol.8:42; vol.10:10, 47; *see also* Architecture, Painting, Sculpture

Asia vol.1:34; vol.4:25; *see also* Continent

Astronaut vol.1:32; vol.10:46

Astronomy vol.9:12, 23

Astrophysicist vol.10:45

Atacama Desert vol.3:41; Index:8

Atlantic Ocean vol.8:29, 44; vol.12:17, 29

Atlas Mountains vol.1:8

Atmosphere vol.4:7

Atom vol.7:23

Atomic bomb vol.12:42

Australia vol.1:5, 35; vol.3:34; vol.4:45; Index:4, 8, 14; *see also* Aborigines, Australia and Oceania, Marsupial

Australia and Oceania vol.1:36; *see also* Aborigines, Australia, Continent, Marsupial

Austria vol.1:37; vol.12:41; *see also* Europe

Ayers Rock vol.1:36

Aztecs vol.1:38; vol.5:29; vol.7:30; Index:13; *see also* Maya, Mexico

B

Babbage, Charles vol.3:8

Baboon vol.7:40

Bach, Johann Sebastian vol.3:6

Bacteria vol.1:39; vol.11:35; *see also* Virus

Badger vol.1:40; *see also* Mammal

Baekeland, Leo Hendrik vol.9:14

Bagpipes vol.12:34

Bahamas vol.1:41; vol.3:15; *see also* Island, North America

Baird, John Logie vol.11:26

Balalaika vol.8:36

Bald eagle vol.1:42; *see also* Eagle

Ballet vol.1:43; vol.3:33; vol.11:31; *see also* Dance

Balloon vol.1:44; vol.8:16; vol.12:30; *see also* Airplane, Transportation

Bamboo vol.8:45; vol.11:12

Banana vol.3:23, 39; vol.5:34; vol.6:18; vol.8:46; vol.9:26; vol.10:5, 7; vol.12:13

Bangladesh vol.1:45; *see also* Asia

Bar Code vol.1:46; *see also* Computer, Laser

Barbados vol.1:47; *see also* Hurricane, North America

Barge vol.1:48; *see also* River, Transportation, Waterway

Bartering vol.7:39

Basketball vol.8:27; vol.9:8

Basketmaker people vol.12:11

Bassoon vol.12:34

Bastille Day vol.4:48

Bat vol.2:4; vol.5:28; vol.7:19; *see also* Mammal

Battle of the Little Bighorn vol.7:41; vol.10:26; Index:16

Battle of Yorktown vol.1:18; vol.12:18

Bay vol.2:5; vol.9:39; *see also* Coast, Ocean, Port, Lake

Bay Island vol.5:34

Bazaar vol.7:44; vol.11:22

Bear vol.1:12, 28, 34; vol.2:6; vol.5:28; vol.7:19; vol.8:21; vol.12:45; *see also* Mammal

Beaver vol.2:7; *see also* Mammal

Bedouin vol.6:23

Bee vol.2:8; *see also* Insect

Beetle vol.2:9; vol.4:33; vol.6:5, 36; *see also* Earwig, Insect

Belgium vol.2:10; vol.6:4; vol.12:42; *see also* Europe

Belize vol.2:11; *see also* Maya, North America

Bell, Alexander Graham vol.3:17; vol.11:25

Bellamy, Francis vol.9:16

Berlin Wall Index:15

Bible vol.2:4, 29; vol.3:4; vol.11:48

Bicycle vol.2:12; vol.3:34, 40; vol.7:48; vol.11:40; vol.12:44; *see also* Motorcycle, Transportation

Bidpai vol.4:28

Bill of Rights vol.3:20, 35

Binary vol.8:27

Bird vol.1:20; vol.2:13; vol.4:13; vol.7:4; vol.8:46; vol.9:44; vol.10:16; vol.12:15, 26; *see also* Animal, Seabird

Bison vol.2:14, 41; vol.8:9, 10; vol.10:43; vol.12:45; *see also* Buffalo, Mammal

Black Hills vol.10:43

Black Sea vol.2:24; vol.12:7

Blackbeard vol.1:41

Blarney Castle vol.6:11

Blood vol.2:15; vol.5:24, 37; vol.7:12; *see also* Heart, Human Body

Blue Ridge Mountains vol.5:8

Bluegrass Region vol.6:29

Bolivia vol.2:16; *see also* South America

Boomerang vol.1:5

Borneo vol.7:18

Bosnia-Herzegovina vol.2:17; vol.10:20; *see also* Serbia and Montenegro

Boston (Massachusetts) vol.5:45; vol.7:23

Boston Tea Party vol.3:12; Index:16

Botanist vol.9:13

Botswana vol.2:18; *see also* Africa

Brachiosaurus vol.2:19; vol.3:42; *see also* Dinosaur, Fossil

Braille vol.11:38

Brazil vol.2:20; vol.9:33; Index:4; *see also* Rain Forest, South America

Breathing vol.1:9, 19; vol.5:37; vol.7:12; vol.9:13; vol.12:19

Bridge vol.7:31

Britain *see* Great Britain

Bronze vol.7:27; vol.12:17; Index:12

Bronze Age vol.2:21; vol.6:12; vol.8:26; *see also* Iron Age, Stone Age

Buddhism vol.2:22, 48; vol.5:46; vol.11:30; Index:12; *see also* India

Buffalo vol.2:14, 23, 41; vol.11:30; *see also* Bison, Mammal

Bulgaria vol.2:24; *see also* Europe

Bus vol.2:25; vol.4:22; vol.11:40; *see also* Transportation

Bush, George H.W. vol.2:26

Bush, George W. vol.2:26; *see also* Iraq

Butterfly vol.2:27, 39; vol.5:28; vol.7:28; vol.10:25; *see also* Caterpillar, Metamorphosis

 C

Cactus vol.2:28; vol.3:41; *see also* Desert, Plant

Cahokia vol.5:43

Calendar vol.2:29; vol.7:25; *see also* Season, Time

California vol.2:30; vol.4:8, 17; Index:18; *see also* Earthquake

Calorie vol.8:28

Cambodia vol.2:31; *see also* Asia

Camel vol.2:32; vol.3:41; vol.10:7, 38; vol.11:17, 47; *see also* Desert, Mammal

Camera vol.2:33; *see also* Light

Canada vol.2:34; vol.3:34; vol.8:17; vol.11:45; Index:4, 8-9; *see also* North America

Canal vol.1:48; vol.12:29

Canoe vol.2:35; *see also* Native Americans, Transportation

Cape Canaveral vol.4:40

Cape Cod vol.6:28; vol.7:23; vol.9:4

Cape Town (South Africa) vol.1:8

Capitol Building vol.6:43; vol.12:24

Capitol Hill vol.3:8

Car vol.2:36; vol.4:22; vol.7:31; vol.11:40; Index:13; *see also* Engine, Transportation

Carat vol.7:26

Carbon dioxide vol.1:9; vol.5:37; vol.7:12; vol.8:41; vol.9:9, 13; vol.11:41

Caribbean vol.3:15, 45; vol.5:20, 34; vol.6:18; vol.8:21; vol.11:43;

Caribou deer vol.1:22, 28; vol.3:36; vol.11:46

Carnivore vol.4:44; vol.11:35

Carthage vol.11:47

Cascade Mountains vol.12:23

Caspian Sea vol.4:25

Castle vol.2:37; vol.6:11; vol.7:32; vol.8:25; *see also* Middle Ages

Cat vol.2:38; vol.4:44; vol.10:7; *see also* Cheetah, Jaguar, Leopard, Lion, Tiger

Caterpillar vol.2:27, 39; vol.7:28, 47; *see also* Butterfly, Metamorphosis, Moth

Cathedral vol.2:40; vol.3:4; vol.7:32; vol.10:47; *see also* Christianity, Middle Ages

Cattle vol.1:29, 31; vol.2:14, 23, 41; vol.8:10, 19, 25, 37; vol.10:4, 31, 43; vol.11:20, 21, 27, 29; vol.12:13, 14, 45, 48; *see also* Farming, Mammal

Cave vol.6:29

CD vol.6:39; vol.7:9

Celtic people vol.11:21

Centipede vol.2:42; *see also* Invertebrate

Central Park vol.8:17

Chad vol.2:43; *see also* Africa

Chalk vol.4:46; vol.9:43

Chameleon vol.7:10

Charlemagne vol.7:32

Cheddar vol.4:23

Cheese vol.4:23; vol.5:7; vol.8:12; vol.11:21; vol.12:35

Cheetah vol.2:44; vol.8:38; *see also* Cat, Mammal

Cherokee people vol.8:22, 32

Chesapeake Bay vol.7:22; vol.12:18

Chewing gum vol.5:18

Cheyenne people vol.7:41; vol.10:26

Chickasaw people vol.8:32

Chicken vol.2:45; vol.4:13; vol.10:42; vol.11:27; vol.12:7; *see also* Bird

Chile vol.2:46; vol.3:41; vol.5:44; Index:8; see also South America

Chimpanzee vol.1:26

China vol.2:12, 47, 48; vol.6:4, 12; vol.8:34; Index:4, 7, 12, 13, 15; see also Asia; China, Ancient

China, Ancient vol.2:48; vol.11:23; vol.12:29; see also Buddhism, China

Chiton vol.7:38

Chocolate vol.2:10; vol.11:21

Choctaw people vol.8:32

Christianity vol.2:40; vol.3:4; vol.5:20; vol.7:32; vol.8:44; vol.9:8: vol.12:13; see also Cathedral, Israel

Christmas vol.5:32; vol.11:20; vol.12:13

Church vol.2:4, 40; vol.3:4

Cinco de Mayo vol.5:32

Civil rights vol.1:11; vol.6:25, 28, 31

Civil War vol.1:11; vol.3:5; vol.7:7; vol.10:29, 42; vol.11:9, 29, 45; vol.12:18, 31; Index:16; see also Lincoln, Abraham; Slavery

Clam vol.7:38

Clarinet vol.12:34

Classical music vol.3:6; vol.8:36; vol.9:6; see also Music, Musical Instrument

Clatsop people vol.6:45

Climate vol.3:7; see also Season, Weather

Clinton, Bill vol.3:8

Clock vol.11:33; Index:12

Coal vol.2:10; vol.4:17, 21, 46; vol.5:6; vol.6:4; vol.7:34; vol.8:23; vol.9:18; vol.10:4, 31; vol.12:11, 18, 31, 45

Coast vol.3:9; see also Bay, Delta

Coast Ranges vol.12:23

Cockerell, Christopher vol.5:36

Cockroach vol.3:10; see also Insect

Cocoa vol.5:10, 20; vol.7:18, 39; vol.8:20, 46; vol.11:43

Cod fish vol.4:13, 34

Coffee vol.3:11, 23; vol.4:16, 24; vol.5:20, 34; vol.6:18, 30; vol.7:15, 30; vol.8:19, 46; vol.9:26; vol.10:5; vol.11:43; vol.12:6, 13

Colombia vol.3:11; see also South America

Colonial America vol.1:6, 18; vol.3:12, 35, 37; vol.5:4, 8, 45; vol.6:46; vol.10:29;vol.12:18, 25; see also American Revolution, Columbus, Christopher

Color vol.3:13; vol.9:34; vol.10:28; vol.11:26; vol.12:26; see also Light

Colorado vol.3:14; see also United States of America

Colorado River vol.12:12

Columbia River vol.8:37

Columbus, Christopher vol.3:12, 15, 31, 45; vol.5:32; vol.9:16; vol.12:13, 17; Index:16; see also Bahamas, Colonial America, Cuba, Venezuela

Comanche people vol.6:27

Comedy vol.3:47

Comet vol.3:16; vol.7:29; vol.10:37, 45; see also Solar System

Commonwealth vol.12:8

Communication vol.3:17; vol.6:6, 38, 39; see also Computer, Internet, Radio, Telephone, Television

Communism vol.5:14; vol.8:24

Compass vol.7:16, 33; Index:13

Composer vol.3:6; vol.8:36

Computer vol.1:46; vol.2:33; vol.3:17, 18; vol.6:6; vol.7:16, 44; vol.8:14, 27, 36; vol.9:42; vol.10:25, 46; vol.11:25; vol.12:30; Index:14; see also Bar Code, Laser

Condor vol.10:41

Confederacy vol.1:11; vol.3:5; vol.11:29

Confucius vol.2:48; vol.8:24

Congress vol.4:26; vol.6:43; vol.12:24

Connecticut vol.3:19; vol.7:23; see also United States of America

Constellation vol.11:7

Constitution vol.1:25; vol.3:20, 35, 37; vol.4:26; vol.5:4; vol.6:25, 43; vol.9:16; vol.12:25; see also Executive Branch, Government, Judicial Branch, Legislative Branch

Constitutional Convention vol.3:20

Continent vol.1:22; vol.3:21; see also Earth, Ocean

Continental Congress vol.3:35

Copernicus, Nicolaus vol.10:37

Copper vol.1:30; vol.7:27, 34; vol.8:19, 46; vol.9:43; vol.11:13; vol.12:6, 11, 35, 46

Coral vol.1:47; vol.3:22; vol.4:35; vol.6:14; vol.7:15; vol.9:18; vol.10:13; see also Coast, Island

Corinth Canal vol.12:29

Cork vol.9:23

Cormorant vol.10:16

Corn vol.2:20; vol.3:11, 23, 29, 37; vol.4:16; vol.6:8; vol.7:36; vol.8:10, 19; vol.9:8, 44: vol.10:30; vol.11:30; vol.12:13, 46, 48

Cornu, Paul vol.5:27

Cortez, Hernando vol.1:38

Costa Rica vol.3:23; see also North America

Cotton vol.1:30, 31, 34; vol.2:43; vol.3:27, 29; vol.6:4; vol.7:30, 36; vol.8:19, 20; vol.9:13; vol.10:20, 29, 41; vol.11:22, 27, 29, 30, 48; vol.12:6, 48

Count Dracula vol.9:44

Cow see Cattle

Coyote vol.3:24; see also Dog, Mammal, Wolf

Crab vol.3:25, 30; vol.6:7; see also Crustacean, Invertebrate, Sea Life

Crafts vol.12:14, 31, 48

Crane vol.3:26; see also Bird

Crater vol.7:29, 42

Crater Lake vol.8:37

Credit card vol.7:39

Creek people vol.8:32

Creole vol.2:11; vol.5:20

Crete Index:12

Cricket (sport) vol.4:23

Croatia vol.3:27; vol.10:20; see also Europe, Serbia and Montenegro

Crocodile vol.1:36; vol.3:28; vol.4:13; vol.9:37; vol.12:46; see also Alligator, Reptile

Crop vol.3:29; vol.4:14, 30, 41; vol.7:44; vol.12:12; see also Farming

Cropover vol.1:47

Crustacean vol.3:25, 30; vol.10:13; see also Animal, Invertebrate, Sea Life

Cuba vol.3:31; see also Island, North America

Cuneiform vol.7:9

Curie, Marie Index:14

Cuttlefish vol.7:38

Cyrillic vol.2:17

Czech Republic vol.3:32; vol.10:30; see also Europe, Slovakia

Czechoslovakia vol.10:30; vol.12:42

D

Da Vinci, Leonardo vol.8:42

Dakota people vol.8:23

Dallas (Texas) vol.6:28

Dam vol.4:17, 39; vol.12:27

Dance vol.1:43, 47; vol.2:20; vol.3:31, 33, 45, 47; vol.5:20, 34; vol.6:11, 30, 47; vol.8:18, 24, 46; vol.9:7, 23; vol.10:47; vol.11:6, 30; see also Ballet, Music

Danube River vol.5:39; vol.9:44

Darling River vol.1:36

Day and Night vol.3:34; vol.11:33; see also Season

Dead Sea vol.6:23

Death Valley vol.2:30; vol.8:21; Index:20

Decimal vol.8:27

Declaration of Independence vol.1:6, 18; vol.3:35; vol.5:4; vol.6:21, 46; vol.9:5; see also American Revolution; Independence Day; Jefferson, Thomas

Deer vol.1:12; vol.3:36; vol.4:25; vol.7:43; vol.9:44; vol.11:46; see also Antelope, Mammal, Moose

Delaware vol.3:37; *see also* United States of America
Delaware people vol.5:47
Delaware River vol.1:18
Delta vol.3:38; vol.7:36; *see also* Coast, River
Democracy vol.5:14
Democratic Republic of Congo vol.3:39; *see also* Africa
Denmark vol.3:40; vol.12:17, 42; *see also* Europe
Desert vol.1:8, 14, 36; vol.2:28, 32, 46; vol.3:41; vol.8:21; vol.10:7, 18; vol.11:17; Index:6, 7; *see also* Cactus, Camel, Climate
Dhow vol.6:35
Diamond vol.1:31; vol.7:26, 34
Didgeridoo vol.12:34
Digestive system vol.5:37
Digital technology vol.2:33
Dingo vol.1:36; vol.3:43
Dinosaur vol.2:19; vol.3:42; vol.4:46; vol.8:15; vol.9:25; vol.11:11, 42; vol.12:5, 11, 15; *see also* Brachiosaurus, Fossil
Disease vol.3:29; vol.4:38, 42; vol.5:7; vol.7:45; vol.9:35; vol.12:19; Index:13
Disney World vol.4:40
Divali vol.5:30
Dog vol.3:24, 43, 48; vol.10:33; vol.12:15; *see also* Coyote, Mammal, Wolf
Dolphin vol.3:44; *see also* Mammal, Sea Life, Whale
Dominican Republic vol.3:45; *see also* Island, North America
Dove vol.9:11
Dragonfly vol.3:46; *see also* Insect
Drakensberg Mountains vol.1:8
Drama vol.3:47; *see also* Literature
Drought vol.4:24
Drug vol.3:48; Index:14
Duck vol.4:4; *see also* Bird, Goose, Swan
Dung beetle vol.2:9

E

E-mail vol.3:17; vol.6:6; vol.11:25
Eagle vol.1:42; vol.4:5; *see also* Bald Eagle, Bird, Hawk
Ear vol.4:6; vol.10:39; *see also* Human Body, Sound
Earth vol.3:34; vol.4:7, 8; vol.9:12; vol.10:37; vol.11:7, 33; vol.12:27; Index:4–9; *see also* Planet, Solar System, Weather
Earthquake vol.2:30; vol.4:8; vol.6:19; vol.7:37; vol.9:7; *see also* California, Earth

Earwig vol.4:9; *see also* Insect
Easter vol.3:4; vol.9:7; vol.12:13
Echolocation vol.2:4; vol.3:44
Ecuador vol.4:10; vol.5:44; *see also* Incas, South America
Edison, Thomas vol.4:11, 17; *see also* Electricity
Eel vol.4:12; *see also* Fish, Sea Life
Egg vol.2:18; vol.4:13, 19; vol.6:32; vol.7:19; vol.8:38; *see also* Bird
Egypt vol.3:38; vol.4:14; *see also* Africa; Egypt, Ancient; Pyramid
Egypt, Ancient vol.4:14, 15; vol.5:29; vol.7:26, 27; vol.9:28; vol.10:23; Index:13; *see also* Egypt, Hieroglyphics, Pyramid
Eiffel Tower vol.4:48
Einstein, Albert Index:14
El Salvador vol.4:16; *see also* North America
Election vol.5:14; vol.6:43
Electricity vol.4:11, 17, 21, 22; vol.5:6, 22; vol.7:5, 6, 27, 34; vol.8:4; vol.9:40; vol.11:25, 39, 44; vol.12:27, 28, 30; *see also* Energy, Heat, Light
Elephant vol.4:6, 18; vol.5:31; vol.11:6; vol.12:46; *see also* Mammal
Elk vol.12:45
Emancipation Proclamation vol.7:7; vol.10:29
Emu vol.4:19; *see also* Australia, Bird
Endangered Species vol.4:18, 20; vol.5:48; vol.8:45; vol.10:5; vol.12:37; *see also* Animal, Plant
Energy vol.4:17, 21, 44; vol.5:6, 22; vol.7:48; vol.8:28; vol.12:28, 30; *see also* Electricity, Heat, Light, Sound
Engine vol.2:36; vol.4:22; vol.7:48; vol.11:39, 40, 44; Index:14; *see also* Car, Electricity, Transportation
England vol.4:23; vol.12:8; *see also* Northern Ireland, Scotland, United Kingdom, Wales
ENIAC vol.3:18
Equator vol.10:18
Erosion vol.3:9; vol.10:36
Ethiopia vol.4:24; vol.5:33; *see also* Africa
Eucalyptus vol.4:45; vol.6:34
Euphrates River vol.6:10
Europe vol.3:21; vol.4:25; vol.6:12; vol.7:32; vol.12:17, 41; Index:7; *see also* Continent
Everglades vol.4:40
Executive Branch vol.4:26; *see also* Constitution, Government, Judicial Branch, Legislative Branch
Exoskeleton vol.10:27

Extinction vol.3:42; vol.4:20
Eye vol.4:27; vol.11:18; *see also* Animal, Human Body

F

Fable vol.4:28; *see also* Legend, Literature, Myth, Story
Factory vol.6:4, 19; vol.7:31; vol.9:5, 42, 44; vol.10:44; vol.12:23, 38
Fairy tale vol.3:40; vol.4:29; *see also* Fable, Literature, Myth, Story
Farming vol.2:41; vol.3:29, 37; vol.4:30, 39; vol.5:48; vol.6:8, 27; vol.7:36; vol.10:36; vol.12:20, 23, 35; *see also* Crop, Soil, Weather
Fax vol.3:17
Federalism vol.5:14
Fenelon Place Elevator vol.6:8
Fern vol.4:31, 45; vol.9:13, 33; *see also* Plant
Ferry vol.10:23
Festival *see* Calendar, and entries for individual countries and religions
Film vol.3:47
Finland vol.4:32; *see also* Arctic, Europe
Firefly vol.4:33; *see also* Beetle, Insect
Fish vol.1:20; vol.4:13, 32, 34, 35, 46; vol.11:38; vol.12:15; *see also* Fish, Tropical; Sea Life
Fish, tropical vol.4:35; *see also* Coral, Fish, Sea Life
Fishing vol.1:12; vol.3:9; vol.5:41; vol.6:19; vol.7:22; vol.8:26, 37; vol.9:39; vol.10:23; vol.11:23
Flag vol.1:12, 17, 31; vol.4:36; vol.10:7; vol.12:9, 10; *see also* American Flag, Communication
Flag Day vol.5:32
Flamenco vol.8:6; vol.10:47
Flamingo vol.4:37; *see also* Bird
Flax vol.2:10, 34; vol.3:29; vol.8:25
Flea vol.4:38; *see also* Insect
Flood vol.1:45; vol.2:31; vol.3:38; vol.4:14, 15, 39; vol.11:48; *see also* Delta, River, Weather
Florida vol.3:12; vol.4:40; *see also* United States of America
Flower vol.2:10; vol.4:41; vol.7:4; vol.8:12; vol.9:13; vol.10:19; vol.11:12; *see also* Leaf, Plant, Seed, Stem
Flute vol.12:34
Fly vol.4:42; *see also* Insect, Mosquito
Folk music vol.4:43; vol.8:6; vol.9:18, 23; vol.10:30; *see also* Music, Musical Instrument
Fontaine, Jean de la vol.4:28
Food vol.3:29; vol.4:30, 44; vol.7:5; vol.8:28, 31; vol.10:20; vol.11:24, 35
Food chain vol.4:44; vol.6:40; vol.9:9; *see also* Animal, Plant

Ford, Henry vol.2:36
Forest vol.4:16, 45; vol.11:30, 41;
    vol.12:23, 46; see also Rain Forest,
    Tree, Wood
Fort Knox vol.6:29
Fort McHenry vol.11:9
Fossil vol.3:42; vol.4:46; vol.9:25;
    vol.12:11; see also Dinosaur, Fuel
Fox vol.4:47; vol.10:28; vol.11:46;
    see also Coyote, Dog, Wolf
France vol.4:48; vol.6:4; vol.11:10, 29,
    39; vol.12:16, 17, 41, 42;
    see also Europe
Franklin, Benjamin vol.4:17; vol.5:4;
    vol.7:6; see also Constitution,
    Lightning
French horn vol.12:34
French Revolution vol.4:48
Frog vol.1:19; vol.5:5, 28; vol.12:26;
    see also Amphibian,
    Metamorphosis, Toad
Fruit vol.9:13
Fuel vol.4:21, 22; vol.5:6, 25, 36;
    vol.7:5, 34; vol.8:28, 41; vol.12:38;
    see also Electricity, Energy, Fossil
Fungus vol.5:7; see also Plant

Gabo, Naum vol.1:33
Gagarin, Yuri vol.10:46; Index:15
Galapagos Islands vol.4:10; vol.9:37
Gamelan music vol.8:6, 36
Ganges River vol.1:34; vol.3:38;
    vol.5:46
Gas vol.1:12; vol.7:34; vol.8:26, 32
Gaucho vol.1:29
Gemini 8 vol.1:32
Geologist vol.3:21
Georgia vol.5:8; see also United States
    of America
Germany vol.5:9; vol.6:4; vol.12:41,
    42; see also Europe
Geyser vol.5:41; vol.12:45
Ghana vol.5:10; see also Africa
Giant's Causeway vol.8:25
Gibbon vol.1:26
Gilbert and Sullivan vol.8:34
Gillespie, Dizzy vol.8:6
Giraffe vol.5:11; vol.12:46;
    see also Mammal
Glacier vol.2:34; vol.5:41
Glass vol.3:32
Goat vol.4:25; vol.5:12; vol.10:7, 31,
    38; vol.12:48; see also Mammal
Gold vol.6:29; vol.7:27, 34; vol.8:13,
    19, 46; vol.9:43; vol.10:43; vol.12:6
Gold Coast vol.5:10
Golden Gate Bridge vol.2:36
Goose vol.5:13; vol.10:15; see also Bird
Gorilla vol.1:26; vol.10:5

Gourd vol.5:20
Government vol.3:20, 35; vol.4:26;
    vol.5:14; vol.6:25, 43; vol.7:22;
    vol.12:8, 18, 24; Index:22, 26-28, 29;
    see also Constitution, Executive
    Branch, Judicial Branch, Legislative
    Branch
Grain vol.2:43; vol.3:27, 29; vol.8:20;
    vol.9:18, 23; vol.10:19, 20, 40;
    vol.11:22
Grand Canyon vol.1:30; vol.12:10, 12
Grand Ole Opry vol.11:27
Grand Teton National Park vol.12:45
Grasshopper vol.4:6; vol.5:15; vol.7:4, 28;
    see also Insect
Gravity vol.10:37; vol.11:18
Great Barrier Reef vol.3:22; vol.6:22
Great Britain vol.4:23; vol.6:4; see
    United Kingdom
Great Depression vol.9:46; Index:17
Great Dividing Range vol.1:36
Great Lakes vol.7:31, 35; vol.8:21, 31;
    vol.12:35
Great Plains vol.6:27; vol.7:41;
    vol.8:10, 16, 23; vol.10:43; Index:20
Great Rift Valley see Rift Valley
Great Salt Lake vol.6:37; vol.12:11
Great Seal vol.1:42
Great Wall of China vol.2:47, 48;
    Index:13
Greece vol.5:16; vol.12:29; see also
    Europe; Greece, Ancient
Greece, Ancient vol.1:16; vol.5:17;
    vol.6:12; vol.8:8, 33; vol.10:10;
    vol.11:31; see also Greece, Olympic
    Games
Green Mountains vol.12:14
Greenland vol.1:28; vol.6:14; Index:4
Grimm, Jacob vol.4:29
Grimm, Wilhelm vol.4:29
Guatemala vol.5:18; see also Maya,
    North America
Guitar vol.8:7; vol.9:20; vol.11:15
Gulf of Mexico vol.7:11, 30, 36;
    vol.8:21
Gulf Stream vol.5:41; vol.8:29
Gull vol.5:19; vol.10:16; vol.12:11, 15;
    see also Bird, Seabird
Gulliver's Travels vol.11:14
Gunpowder vol.2:48
Guru Nanak vol.10:24

Haiti vol.5:20; see also North America
Hale, Nathan vol.3:19
Hale-Bopp comet vol.3:16
Haley, Bill vol.9:20
Halley's Comet vol.3:16; Index:15
Hansel and Gretel vol.4:29
Hanson vol.9:20

Harbor vol.3:9, 40; vol.6:41; vol.7:22;
    vol.9:22
Hare vol.5:21; see also Mammal,
    Rabbit
Hartford (Connecticut) vol.3:19
Harvard University vol.7:23; vol.9:46
Hawaii vol.5:22; vol.6:14; vol.12:20;
    see also United States of America
Hawk vol.5:23; see also Bird
Heart vol.2:15; vol.5:24, 37;
    see also Blood, Human Body
Heat vol.5:6, 25; vol.7:27, 34;
    vol.11:18; see also Energy, Fuel
Hedgehog vol.5:26, 28; see also
    Hibernation, Mammal
Helicopter vol.5:27; see also Airplane,
    Transportation
Hendrix, Jimi vol.8:7
Henson, Jim vol.9:27
Herbivore vol.4:44; vol.11:35
Hershey chocolate factory vol.9:5
Hibernation vol.2:4; vol.5:5, 26, 28;
    vol.10:18, 35; vol.11:46;
    see also Animal, Season
Hidatsa people vol.6:45; vol.10:6
Hieroglyphics vol.4:15; vol.5:29; vol.7:25;
    see also Alphabet; Aztecs; Egypt,
    Ancient; Maya
Hillary, Sir Edmund vol.8:11
Himalaya Mountains vol.1:34;
    vol.5:46; vol.8:4, 11; Index:6
Hinduism vol.2:29; vol.5:30, 46;
    vol.8:11; see also India
Hippopotamus vol.5:31; vol.12:46;
    see also Mammal
Hispaniola vol.3:44; vol.5:20
Hitler, Adolf vol.12:42
Holiday vol.5:32, 45; see also
    Calendar, Festival, Independence
    Day
Holland vol.8:12
Holocaust vol.6:24
Hologram vol.6:39
Home vol.1:45; vol.2:11, 18, 24, 43;
    vol.5:33, 34, 48; vol.7:18; vol.8:46;
    vol.9:8, 23: vol.10:5, 38, 44;
    vol.11:21; vol.12:38, 48; see also
    Architecture
Honduras vol.5:34; see also North
    America
Hong Kong (China) vol.1:34
Hoover Dam vol.4:17
Hopewell people vol.8:31
Horse vol.5:35; vol.6:29; vol.11:40;
    see also Mammal, Transportation
Horseshoe Falls vol.8:17
Hot Springs National Park vol.1:31
House of Representatives vol.6:43
Hovercraft vol.5:36; see also
    Transportation

Huange He River vol.1:34
Huang River vol.4:39
Hu-hu vol.2:43
Human Body vol.2:15; vol.4:21, 44;
    vol.5:24, 25, 37; vol.7:4, 26;
    vol.8:28, 41; vol.10:27; vol.12:27;
    see also Blood, Heart, Lung
Hummingbird vol.2:13; vol.4:13;
    vol.5:38; vol.10:41; see also Bird,
    Migration
Humus vol.10:36
Hungary vol.5:39; see also Europe
Hurricane vol.1:47; vol.4:40; vol.5:40;
    vol.7:11; vol.11:23; vol.12:30;
    see also Tornado, Weather
Hutu people vol.10:5

Iceberg vol.8:29
Iceland vol.5:41; see also Europe,
    Island
Idaho vol.5:42; see also United States
    of America
Iditerod vol.1:12
Ifugo people vol.9:8
Iguana vol.7:10
Illinois vol.5:43; vol.7:7; see also
    Lincoln, Abraham
Immigration vol.11:10; Index:17
Incas vol.5:44; vol.9:7; see also Aztecs,
    Maya, South America
Independence Day vol.5:32, 45;
    see also American Revolution,
    Declaration of Independence,
    Holiday
India vol.5:46; vol.6:12; vol.8:43;
    vol.10:24; Index:4, 7, 8, 15; see also
    Asia
Indian Ocean vol.8:29
Indian Territory vol.8:32
Indiana vol.5:47; vol.7:7; see also
    United States of America
Indonesia vol.5:48; see also Asia
Indus River vol.8:43
Industrial revolution vol.6:4; vol.7:23;
    Index:13; see also United Kingdom
Indy 500 vol.5:47
Insect vol.1:20; vol.2:27, 39; vol.6:5, 7;
    vol.7:4, 28; see also Animal,
    Invertebrate, Metamorphosis
International Peace Garden vol.8:23
Internet vol.6:6; vol.7:9; vol.11:25;
    see also Communication,
    Computer, Telephone
Inuit people vol.11:46
Invertebrate vol.6:5, 7; vol.7:38;
    see also Crustacean, Insect,
    Mollusk, Vertebrate
Iowa vol.6:8; see also United States
    of America

Iran vol.6:9, 10; Index:15; see also Asia
Iraq vol.2:26; vol.6:10; see also Asia
Ireland vol.5:32; vol.6:11; vol.12:17, 34;
    see also Europe, Northern Ireland
Iron vol.7:16, 27, 35; vol.9:43; vol.12:22
Iron Age vol.2:21; vol.6:12;
    see also Bronze Age, Stone Age
Islam vol.6:9, 13, 23; vol.8:43;
    vol.11:22; see also Iraq, Saudi
    Arabia
Island vol.1:36, 41, 47; vol.3:31, 45;
    vol.5:16, 41, 48; vol.6:14, 18, 19
    vol.7:15, 17; vol.8:18, 46; vol.10:7;
    vol.11:43; see also Coast, Coral,
    Ocean
Israel vol.6:15, 23, 24; see also Asia,
    Judaism
Italy vol.6:16; vol.9:4; vol.12:17, 41, 42;
    see also Europe; Rome, Ancient

J

Jackal vol.3:43
Jackrabbit see Hare
Jaguar vol.6:17; see also Cat, Leopard
Jamaica vol.6:18; see also North
    America
Jamestown (Virginia) vol.3:12;
    vol.12:18; Index:16
Japan vol.6:4, 19; vol.12:42; Index:7;
    see also Asia, Earthquake
Jasper National Park vol.2:34
Jazz vol.6:20; vol.8:6; vol.9:6; see also
    Music, Musical Instrument
Jefferson, Thomas vol.3:35; vol.6:21, 45;
    see also Declaration of
    Independence, Lewis and Clark
Jellyfish vol.6:7, 22; see also
    Invertebrate, Sea Life
Jerusalem vol.6:15, 24
Jesus Christ vol.3:4; Index:13
Jewelry vol.7:34
Jordan vol.6:23; see also Asia
Judaism vol.2:29; vol.6:15, 24; vol.12:34;
    see also Israel
Judicial Branch vol.6:25; see also
    Constitution, Executive Branch,
    Legislative Branch
Junkanoo vol.1:41
Jurassic Period vol.2:19
Jute vol.1:45

K

Kalahari Desert vol.1:8; vol.2:18
Kangaroo vol.1:36; vol.6:26; vol.7:21;
    see also Australia, Mammal,
    Marsupial
Kansas vol.6:25, 27; see also United
    States of America
Karakoram Mountains vol.8:4

Kathak dance vol.3:33
Kazakstan Index:4
Kennedy, John F. vol.3:8; vol.6:28;
    Index:17; see also Clinton, Bill
Kennedy Space Center vol.4:40;
    vol.6:6
Kentucky vol.6:29; vol.7:7; see also
    United States of America
Kenya vol.6:30; vol.12:47; see also
    Africa
Key, Francis Scott vol.11:9; Index:16
Kinetograph vol.4:11
King, Dr. Martin Luther, Jr. vol.5:32;
    vol.6:31; Index:17; see also Holiday
King Arthur vol.6:42
King Christophe of Haiti vol.5:20
Kiwi vol.1:36; vol.6:32; vol.8:18;
    see also Bird, New Zealand
Knight vol.6:33, 42; see also Middle
    Ages
Koala vol.1:36; vol.6:34; vol.7:21;
    see also Australia, Mammal,
    Marsupial
Kobe (Japan) vol.6:19
Komodo dragon vol.5:48; vol.7:10
Koran vol.6:13
Korean War vol.1:32
Krill vol.1:22
Kuala Lumpur vol.6:13
Kuwait vol.5:6; vol.6:10, 35; see also
    Asia, Desert
Kwanzaa vol.5:32

Labor Day vol.5:32
Ladybug vol.4:44; vol.6:36; see also
    Beetle, Insect
Lake vol.2:16, 43; vol.6:23, 37; vol.7:35;
    vol.8:19, 37; vol.11:47; vol.12:11;
    Index:20; see also River, Valley
Lake Baikal vol.1:34
Lake Chad vol.2:43
Lake Champlain vol.12:14
Lake Erie vol.8:31
Lake Michigan vol.5:43; vol.12:35
Lake Titicaca vol.2:16; vol.9:7
Lake Victoria vol.1:8; vol.12:6
Lake Volta vol.5:10
Lakota people vol.8:9; vol.10:26
Language vol.2:17; vol.3:39; vol.6:13,
    38; vol.7:9; vol.9:45; vol.10:31;
    vol.11:13; vol.12:22, 46; see also
    Alphabet, Communication
Lapland vol.4:32; vol.11:46
Laser vol.1:46; vol.6:39; Index:15; see
    also Bar Code, Computer, Light
Lead vol.12:35
Leaf vol.4:31; vol.6:40; vol.9:13;
    vol.11:12, 41; see also
    Photosynthesis, Plant

League of Nations vol.12:33
Leaning Tower of Pisa vol.6:16
Leap year vol.2:29
Lebanon vol.6:41; *see also* Asia
Legend vol.6:42; vol.8:25;
    see also Literature, Myth, Story
Legislative Branch vol.6:43; vol.8:10;
    see also Constitution, Executive
    Branch, Judicial Branch
Lemur vol.7:15
Leopard vol.6:17, 44; *see also* Cat,
    Jaguar, Mammal
Lessing, Gotthold Ephraim vol.4:28
Lever vol.7:14
Lewis and Clark vol.6:45; vol.7:37;
    vol.10:6; Index:16; *see also*
    Jefferson, Thomas; Sacagawea
Liberty Bell vol.6:46; Index:16; *see also*
    Declaration of Independence
Library of Congress vol.6:43
Libya vol.6:47; Index:9; *see also* Africa,
    Desert
Lice vol.3:30; vol.6:48; *see also* Insect
Lichen vol.1:22, 28; vol.5:38; vol.11:46
Life cycle vol.7:4; *see also* Flower,
    Metamorphosis
Light vol.3:13, 17, 34; vol.4:11, 21, 27;
    vol.7:5, 42; vol.9:34; vol.11:18;
    see also Color, Energy, Sun
Lightning vol.7:6; vol.8:8; vol.12:30;
    see also Electricity, Weather
Lincoln, Abraham vol.3:5; vol.5:43;
    vol.7:7; *see also* Civil War
Lion vol.2:38; vol.4:44; vol.7:8; *see also*
    Africa, Cat, Mammal
Literacy vol.7:13, 32
Literature vol.7:9; vol.10:38; *see also*
    Drama, Poetry, Story
Livingstone, David vol.12:46
Lizard vol.1:20; vol.7:10; vol.9:37;
    vol.10:7; vol.12:26; *see also*
    Reptile
Llama vol.4:10; vol.9:7
Lobster vol.3:30; vol.6:7
Loch Ness vol.6:37; vol.10:9
Locust vol.6:5
London (UK) vol.4:23, 39; vol.11:16,
    31; vol.12:8, 42
Long Island vol.8:17
Long Island Sound vol.3:19
Longfellow, Henry Wadsworth vol.9:17
Louisiana vol.5:45; vol.7:11; *see also*
    United States of America
Louisiana Purchase vol.6:21, 45
Louisville vol.6:29
Lumber industry vol.8:37
Lung vol.2:15; vol.5:37; vol.7:12;
    see also Air, Human Body, Oxygen
Luxembourg; vol.7:13; *see also*
    Europe

M

Machine, Simple; vol.7:14; *see also*
    Energy
Machu Picchu (Peru) vol.5:44; Index:13
Mackinac Bridge vol.7:31
Madagascar vol.7:15; *see also* Africa,
    Island
Madison, James vol.3:20
Magnet vol.7:16; *see also* Metal
Maine vol.7:17, 23; *see also* United
    States of America
Malaria vol.4:42
Malaysia vol.7:18; vol.10:18; *see also*
    Asia, Rain Forest
Mali vol.12:9
Mammal vol.1:20; vol.4:13; vol.7:4,
    19, 21; vol.10:13; vol.12:15; *see also*
    Animal, Vertebrate
Mandan people vol.6:45
Mandela, Nelson vol.10:40
Maori people vol.8:8, 18
Map vol.7:20; Index:12
Maple syrup vol.12:14
March on Washington for Jobs and
    Freedom vol.6:31
Marconi, Guglielmo vol.9:31
Mardi Gras vol.7:11
Mariana Trench vol.8:29; Index:6
Mars vol.12:20
Marsh Arabs vol.6:10
Marsupial vol.6:26, 34; vol.7:21; vol.8:35;
    see also Australia, Kangaroo,
    Koala, Mammal, Opossum
Maryland vol.7:22; vol.11:9, 45;
    see also United States of America;
    Washington, D.C.
Massachusetts vol.3:12; vol.7:17, 23;
    vol.9:4; *see also* American
    Revolution, Colonial America
Matter vol.7:24; *see also* Temperature
Maya vol.2:11; vol.5:18, 29; vol.7:25;
    vol.9:28; *see also* Aztecs,
    Hieroglyphics, Incas, Pyramid
McKinley, William vol.9:47
Measurement vol.7:26; vol.11:33;
    see also Calendar, Number, Time
Mecca vol.6:13; vol.10:7
Medicine vol.3:48; vol.5:7, 24; vol.6:39;
    vol.12:19
Mediterranean Sea vol.4:14, 25;
    vol.5:16; vol 9:4
Mekong River vol.2:31
Memorial Day vol.5:32
Memphis (Tennessee) vol.6:31; vol.11:27
Mennonite people vol.9:5
Mesa Verde National Park vol.3:14
Metal vol.2:21; vol.5:25, 42; vol.6:12,
    33, 39; vol.7:27, 34, 39; vol.8:41;
    vol.9:5, 43; vol.10:4; vol.11:13;
    see also Magnet, Meteor, Rock

Metamorphosis vol.1:19; vol.2:27, 39;
    vol.6:5; vol.7:28; *see also*
    Amphibian, Insect, Life Cycle
Meteor vol.7:29; *see also* Earth, Solar
    System
Meteorite vol.7:29
Meteorologist vol.12:30
Metric system vol.7:26
Mexico vol.1:38; vol.5:32; vol.7:25, 30;
    vol.8:21; vol.9:4; vol.11:29;
    Index:12; *see also* Aztecs, Maya,
    North America
Mexico City vol.7: 30; vol.8:21
Miami people vol.5:47
Michigan vol.7:31; *see also* United
    States of America
Middle Ages vol.2:37, 40; vol.6:33;
    vol.7:32; *see also* Castle, Cathedral,
    Knight
Middle East vol.6:12, 13, 15, 23, 35, 41;
    vol.7:9, 20; vol.10:7; vol.11:22, 48
Migration vol.3:26; vol.4:4; vol.5:13,
    38; vol.7:33; vol.11:19; vol.12:32;
    see also Animal
Milne, A. A. vol.9:17
Mining vol.1:30, 31; vol.2:10, 31;
    vol.5:42; vol.7:34, 35, 41; vol.8:13,
    16, 19, 46; vol.9:18; vol.10:4, 20, 31,
    40, 43; vol.11:22; vol.12:6, 7, 11, 18,
    31, 35, 45, 48; *see also* Metal, Rock
Minnesota vol.7:35; *see also* United
    States of America
Mississippi vol.7:36; *see also* Delta,
    United States of America
Mississippi River vol.1:48; vol.3:38;
    vol.4:39; vol.6:8; vol.7:11, 35, 37;
    vol.8:21; Index:20
Missouri vol.7:37; *see also* United
    States of America
Missouri River vol.6:8, 45; vol.7:37;
    Index:20
Model T vol.2:36; Index:14, 17
Mohawk people vol.8:9
Mold *see* Fungus
Mollusk vol.7:38; vol.10:13; *see also*
    Animal, Invertebrate
Monarchy vol.5:14, 44; vol.7:11, 25
Money vol.7:39; *see also* Haiti
Mongols vol.2:48
Monitor lizard vol.7:10
Monkey vol.1:20, 34; vol.7:40;
    vol.10:25, 41; vol.12:16; *see also*
    Ape, Mammal
Monsoon vol.1:45; vol.9:8
Montana vol.4:47; vol.7:41; *see also*
    United States of America
Monteverdi, Claudio vol.8:36
Montgolfier brothers vol.1:44
Montgomery Bus Boycott vol.1:11;
    vol.6:31

Moon vol.1:32; vol.4:40; vol.7:29, 42; Index:15, 17; *see also* Earth, Solar System, Space Exploration, Sun

Moose vol.1:12; vol.7:43; *see also* Arctic, Deer

Mormons vol.12:11

Morocco vol.7:44; *see also* Africa, Desert

Morse code vol.3:17

Moses vol.6:24

Mosque vol.6:9, 10, 13

Mosquito vol.7:45; vol.11:46; *see also* Fly, Insect

Moss vol.1:22, 28; vol.7:46; vol.9:13, 33; vol.11:46; *see also* Plant

Moth vol.2:39; vol.7:47; *see also* Butterfly, Caterpillar, Insect, Metamorphosis

Mother Teresa vol.1:13

Motorcycle vol.7:48; *see also* Bicycle, Transportation

Mount Ararat vol.11:48

Mount Everest vol.1:34; vol.8:11; Index:6

Mount Kilimanjaro vol.1:8

Mount McKinley (Denali) vol.1:12; vol.8:21; Index:20

Mount Rushmore vol.10:43; vol.12:25

Mount St. Helens vol.12:23

Mount Wilhelm vol.1:36

Mountain vol.1:12, 29, 34, 37; vol.2:17, 46; vol.3:14; vol.5:18, 34; vol.6:41; vol.7:41, 42; vol.8:4, 11, 25, 29; vol.10:31; vol.11:21; vol.12:14, 20, 22, 23, 31; Index:6, 7, 9, 20; *see also* Island, Volcano

Mounties vol.2:34

Mouse vol.8:5; *see also* Mammal

Movie vol.2:33; vol.11:31; Index:17

Mozart, Wolfgang Amadeus vol.1:37; vol.8:34

MRI vol.7:16

Mummy vol.7:27; vol.9:28

Mushroom *see* Fungus

Music vol.1:37, 43, 47; vol.2:43; vol.3:6, 23, 31, 33; vol.4:11, 43; vol.5:34, 41, 45; vol.6:11, 18, 20; vol.8:6, 7, 11, 19, 20, 34, 36; vol.9:6, 7, 17, 20, 23; vol.11:9, 15, 27, 41; vol.12:22, 31, 34; *see also* Classical Music, Jazz, Musical Instrument, Percussion Instrument, Stringed Instrument, Wind Instrument

Musical vol.8:34

Musical instrument vol.3:6; vol.4:32, 43; vol.5:41; vol.6:20; vol.8:7, 36; vol.9:6, 20; vol.10:30; vol.12:34, 38; *see also* Music, Percussion Instrument, Stringed Instrument, Wind Instrument

Mycologist vol.5:7

Myth vol.6:42; vol.8:8; *see also* Legend, Literature, Story

National Aeronautics and Space Administration (NASA) vol.1:32

National Air Museum vol.12:44

National Archives vol.3:35; vol.12:24

National Museum of the American Indian vol.12:24

Native Americans vol.1:12, 16, 30, 31, 38; vol.2:35, 46; vol.3:12, 14, 33; vol.4:10; vol.5:42; vol.6:27, 45; vol.7:25, 30, 37, 41; vol.8:8, 9, 10, 16, 19, 21, 22, 23, 32, 44; vol.9:7; vol.10:6, 29, 41; vol.12:10, 13, 45; *see also* North America, Sacagawea

Nautilus vol.11:16

Navaho people vol.1:30; vol.8:16

Nebraska vol.8:10; *see also* United States of America

Nepal vol.2:22; vol.4:30; vol.8:11; *see also* Asia, Mountain

Netherlands vol.8:12; vol.9:22; vol.12:17, 42; *see also* Europe

Nevada vol.8:13; *see also* United States of America

New England vol.3:19; vol.7:23; vol.8:14; vol.12:14

New Hampshire vol.7:23; vol.8:14; *see also* United States of America

New Jersey vol.8:15; vol.12:33; *see also* United States of America

New Mexico vol.8:16; *see also* United States of America

New Orleans vol.6:20; vol.7:11

New Year vol.2:29, 47; vol.5:32; vol.10:25, 38; vol.12:16

New York vol.8:17; vol.9:22; vol.11:10; *see also* Statue of Liberty

New York City vol.4:11; vol.5:33, 45; vol.8:17; vol.12:9; Index:18

New Zealand vol.1:36; vol.8:18; vol.10:22; see also Australia and Oceania, Kiwi

Nez Percé vol.5:42

Niagara Falls vol.8:17, 21

Nicaragua vol.8:19; *see also* North America

Nigeria vol.8:20; *see also* Africa

Nile River vol.1:8; vol.3:38; vol.4:14, 15, 39; vol.12:6; Index:6

Nobel Peace Prize vol.12:33

Nomad vol.5:33; vol.6:9, 23; vol.10:38; vol.11:17

Norgay, Tenzing vol.8:11

Norman Conquest vol.7:32

North America vol.3:12, 21; vol.8:21; vol.11:36; vol.12:17; *see also* Continent, Native Americans

North Carolina vol.5:40; vol.8:22; vol.12:44; *see also* United States of America

North Dakota vol.6:45; vol.8:23; vol.10:6; *see also* United States of America

North Korea vol.8:24; *see also* Asia, South Korea

North Pole vol.1:28; vol.7:16; vol.11:16

Northern Ireland vol.8:25; vol.12:8; *see also* United Kingdom, Europe

Norway vol.8:26; vol.12:17, 42; *see also* Arctic, Europe, Vikings

Nuclear bomb Index:15

Number vol.8:27; *see also* Computer, Money

Nutrient vol.5:37; vol.8:28

Nutrition vol.8:28; *see also* Food Chain, Human Body

Oasis vol.3:41

Oboe vol.12:34

Ocean vol.4:7; vol.8:29, 44; *see also* Water; Index:6

Octopus vol.7:38; vol.8:30; *see also* Mollusk, Squid

Ohio vol.8:31; *see also* United States of America

Oil vol.1:12; vol.3:41; vol.5:6; vol.6:9, 10, 35, 47; vol.7:11, 34; vol.8:20, 23, 26, 29, 32; vol.9:14; vol.10:4, 7; vol.11:22, 29; vol.12:13, 31, 45

Oklahoma vol.8:32; *see also* United States of America

Olmec people Index:12

Olympic Games vol.8:33; vol.10:44; Index:12; *see also* Greece, Ancient

Olympic National Forest vol.12:23

Opera vol.3:6; vol.8:34; vol.11:31; *see also* Drama, Music, Theater

Opossum vol.7:21; vol.8:35; *see also* Mammal, Marsupial

Orangutan vol.1:26

Orchestra vol.3:6; vol.8:34, 36; *see also* Classical Music, Musical Instrument

Oregon vol.8:37; *see also* United States of America

Ornithologist vol.2:13

Osage people vol.6:27

Ostrich vol.2:13, 18; vol.4:13; vol.8:38; *see also* Bird

Otter vol.8:39; *see also* Mammal

Owl vol.4:27; vol.8:40; *see also* Bird

Oxygen vol.1:9; vol.2:15; vol.4:45; vol.5:37; vol.7:12; vol.8:41; vol.9:9, 13; vol.10:13; *see also* Air, Lung, Plant

Oyster vol.7:38

Ozarks vol.1:31; vol.7:37

P

Pacific Ocean vol.6:45; vol.8:29, 44; vol.10:6; vol.12:29; Index:6
Painting vol.1:33; vol.8:12, 42; *see also* Art
Pakistan vol.8:43; *see also* Asia
Palestine vol.6:15
Palm vol.6:40
Pampas vol.1:29; vol.10:41
Panama vol.8:44; *see also* North America, Waterway
Panama Canal vol.8:44; vol.9:47; vol.12:29
Panda vol.8:45; *see also* Mammal
Paper vol.2:48; vol.5:8; vol.9:13, 23; vol.11:20, 41; vol.12:23, 35, 38
Paprika vol.3:32; vol.5:39
Papua New Guinea vol.1:36; vol.8:42, 46; *see also* Australia and Oceania
Parasite vol.3:30
Paris vol.4:48
Parrot vol.8:47; *see also* Bird
Parthenon vol.5:17
Peace Corps vol.6:28
Peanut vol.5:8
Pearl Harbor Index:17
Peary, Robert vol.1:28
Peat vol.5:6; vol.7:46
Penguin vol.1:22; vol.2:13; vol.8:48; *see also* Antarctica, Bird
Penicillin vol.5:7
Peninsula vol.3:37; vol.4:40; vol.7:31; vol.9:4; *see also* Coast
Pennsylvania vol.6:46; vol.9:5; vol.11:45; *see also* Liberty Bell, United States of America
Pentagon vol.12:18
Percussion Instrument vol.8:36; vol.9:6; *see also* Music, Musical Instrument, Orchestra
Perfume vol.4:41
Persia vol.6:9
Peru vol.5:44; vol.9:7; *see also* Incas, South America
Petit Jean State Park vol.1:31
Pharaoh vol.4:15; vol.9:28
Philadelphia vol.6:46; vol.9:5
Philippines vol.9:8; *see also* Asia
Phnom Penh vol.2:31
Phonograph vol.4:11
Photosynthesis vol.6:40; vol.9:9, 13; *see also* Leaf, Plant
Piano vol.9:6
Picasso, Pablo vol.10:47
Pied Piper of Hamelin vol.5:9
Pig vol.9:10; *see also* Mammal
Pigeon vol.9:11; *see also* Bird
Pilbra ningaui vol.7:21
Pilgrimage vol.6:13

Piranha vol.4:35
Pitcher plant vol.4:20
Plains Indians vol.8:10, 23
Planet vol.4:7; vol.7:42; vol.9:12; vol.10:37, 45, 46; *see also* Solar System, Sun
Plankton vol.10:13
Plant vol.2:28; vol.3:29, 48; vol.4:41, 44; vol.6:40; vol.7:4; vol.9:9, 13, 48; vol.10:19, 36; vol.11:12, 18; vol.12:27, 28; Index:10-11; *see also* Flower, Food Chain, Leaf, Life Cycle, Photosynthesis, Seed, Stem
Plantain vol.3:23; vol.12:6
Plantation vol.3:5; vol.5:34; vol.6:18; vol.7:36; vol.10:29, 42
Plastic vol.5:25; vol.9:13; vol.11:25; *see also* Heat
Platypus vol.9:15; *see also* Australia, Mammal
Pledge of Allegiance vol.9:16
Poetry vol.4:32; vol.7:9; vol.9:17; vol.12:22; *see also* Literature
Poland vol.9:18, 19; vol.12:42; *see also* Europe
Polar bear vol.2:6
Polder vol.8:12
Police vol.4:23
Pollen vol.4:41
Pollution vol.1:9; vol.2:36; vol.4:22; vol.7:12; vol.8:29; vol.9:19, 41, 44; *see also* Air, Ocean, Road
Poor Richard's Almanack vol.5:4
Pop music vol.9:6, 20; vol.10:30; *see also* Music, Musical Instrument
Population, world Index:7, 12, 13
Porcupine vol.9:21; *see also* Mammal
Port vol.3:27; vol.8:12, 31; vol.9:22; vol.10:25, 42; vol.11:27; vol.12:23, 35; *see also* Bay, Coast, Ship
Portugal vol.9:23; *see also* Europe
Possum vol.7:21; vol.8:35
Potassium vol.7:27
Potato vol.2:16; vol.9:7, 18; vol.10:4, 20, 31; vol.11:12; vol.12:23
Potawatomi vol.5:47
Potomac River vol.12:24
Praying Mantis vol.9:24; *see also* Insect, Invertebrate
President vol.1:6; vol.2:26; vol.3:8; vol.4:26; vol.6:21, 28; vol.7:7; vol.9:46, 47; vol.10:43; vol.12:18, 25, 33; Index:22, 26-28, 29
Presidents Day vol.5:32
Princeton University vol.12:33
Printing vol.2:48
Pterosaur vol.9:25; *see also* Dinosaur, Fossil
Pueblo Indians vol.8:16
Puerto Rico vol.9:26; *see also* North America, United States of America

Puffin vol.10:15
Pulley vol.7:14
Punch and Judy vol.9:27
Puppetry vol.9:27; *see also* Drama, Theater
Puritan vol.3:12
Pygmy vol.3:39; vol.10:5
Pyramid vol.4:14, 15; vol.7:25; vol.9:28; Index:12; *see also* Egypt; Egypt, Ancient; Maya
Pythagoras vol.8:6

Q

Quaker vol.1:25
Quéchua people vol.4:10; vol.9:7
Quipu vol.5:44

R

Rabbit vol.4:6; vol.9:29; vol.11:46; *see also* Hare, Mammal
Raccoon vol.9:30; vol.10:28; *see also* Mammal
Radio vol.3:17, 47; vol.7:16; vol.9:31; vol.11:25, 26, 27; Index:14; *see also* Communication, Television
Railroad vol.9:32; vol.11:39; vol.12:12; Index:16; *see also* Train, Transportation
Rain vol.12:28, 30; Index:8
Rain forest vol.1:8, 34; vol.2:20; vol.3:39; vol.4:45; vol.5:18, 48; vol.7:15, 18; vol.8:21, 44; vol.9:33; vol.10:18, 41; vol.11:17; vol.12:13, 16, 23; *see also* Forest, Plant
Rainbow vol.9:34; *see also* Color, Light
Ramp vol.7:14
Rastafarianism vol.2:29
Rat vol.3:41; vol.8:5; vol.9:35; *see also* Mammal
Ray vol.9:36; *see also* Fish, Sea Life
Recycling vol.9:14
Red Sea vol.4:14
Red Square vol.10:4
Reggae vol.6:18
Reindeer vol.1:28; vol.4:32
Religion vol.2:22, 29, 40; vol.3:4, 12, 33; vol.4:15, 16; vol.5:17, 20, 30, 32, 44, 46; vol.6:9, 11, 13, 15, 23, 24, 46; vol.7:25; vol.8:8, 11, 33, 43, 44; vol.9:7, 8, 16, 23, 26; vol.10:7, 24; vol.11:30; vol.12:11, 13, 17, 34
Renaissance vol.7:32
Reptile vol.1:15, 20; vol.4:13; vol.5:28; vol.7:4; vol.9:37; vol.12:15; *see also* Animal
Reservation vol.7:41; vol.8:9, 16; vol.10:26, 43
Reservoir vol.8:4; vol.12:27

Rhinoceros vol.4:20; vol.9:38; vol.12:46; see also Mammal

Rhode Island vol.7:23; vol.9:39; Index:18; see also United States of America

Rice vol.1:31, 34; vol.2:31, 47; vol.3:29, 39; vol.4:30; vol.5:46, 48; vol.6:19; vol.7:11, 15, 18, 36; vol.8:11, 24, 43; vol.9:7, 8, 26; vol.10:19, 44; vol.11:6, 23, 30, 43; vol.12:16

Rift Valley vol.6:30, 37

Rio de Janeiro vol.2:20

Rio Grande vol.8:16

River vol.1:45, 48; vol.2:31; vol.3:38; vol.4:39; vol.6:37; vol.8:9, 10; vol.9:40; vol.12:12, 27, 28, 31; Index:20; see also Delta, Flood, Valley

Road vol.9:41, 45; vol.12:12; see also Transportation

Robot vol.9:42; vol.10:45; see also Laser, Space Exploration

Rock vol.4:7, 46; vol.7:27, 34; vol.8:4, 25; vol.9:43; vol.12:11, 20; see also Metal, Mining

Rocky Mountains vol.3:14; vol.5:42; vol.7:41; vol.8:21; vol.12:10, 45; Index:20

Rodeo vol.12:45

Roman Catholicism vol.6:11, 16; vol.9:7, 26

Romania vol.9:44; see also Europe

Rome, Ancient vol.1:16; vol.4:15; vol.5:17; vol.7:32; vol.8:8, 33; vol.9:41, 45; vol.10:10, 29; Index:12, 13; see also Italy, Road

Rome vol.6:16; vol.9:45

Roosevelt, Franklin D. vol.9:46

Roosevelt, Theodore vol.9:46, 47; see also Roosevelt, Franklin D.

Root vol.9:9, 13, 48; vol.10:19; vol.11:12; see also Plant

Rosh Hashanah vol.12:34

Rotterdam (Netherlands) vol.8:12; vol.9:22

Rubber tapping vol.2:20; vol.7:18; vol.11:41

Ruby vol.7:34

Rugby vol.4:23; vol.12:22

Russia vol.6:4; vol.10:4; vol.12:41, 42; Index:4, 14; see also Asia, Europe

Rwanda vol.9:6; vol.10:5; see also Africa

S

Sacagawea vol.6:45; vol.10:6; see also Lewis and Clark

Safari vol.6:30

Sahara Desert vol.1:8, 14; vol.3:41; Index:6

St. Patrick's Day vol.5:32; vol.6:11

Salmon vol.7:33

Salt vol.7:34; vol.12:11; vol.12:27, 31

Salt Lake City vol.12:11

Samburu tribe vol.6:30

San Francisco (California) vol.2:5, 36

San people vol.2:18

Santa Fe (New Mexico) vol.8:16

Satellite vol.3:17; vol.9:31; vol.10:45, 46; vol.11:25, 26; vol.12:30

Saturn vol.7:42

Saudi Arabia vol.3:41; vol.6:13; vol.10:7; see also Asia, Islam

Savanna vol.1:8

Saxophone vol.12:34

School of the Air vol.1:35

Scorpion vol.3:41; vol.10:8; see also Invertebrate

Scotland vol.6:37; vol.10:9; vol.12:8, 34; see also Europe, United Kingdom

Screw vol.7:14

Sculpture vol.1:33; vol.5:22; vol.10:10; see also Art

Sea Index:6

Sea Anemone vol.10:11; see also Sea Life

Sea Horse vol.10:12; see also Fish

Sea Islands vol.5:8; vol.10:42

Sea Life vol.3:44; vol.10:13; see also Coral, Fish

Sea Lion vol.10:14; see also Mammal, Sea Life

Sea Urchin vol.10:15; see also Sea Life

Seabird vol.5:19; vol.10:13, 16; see also Bird, Gull

Seal vol.1:22, 28; vol.10:17; see also Mammal, Sea Lion

Season vol.1:45; vol.3:7, 34; vol.10:18; vol.11:30, 33, 43; vol.12:13, 14, 28, 46; Index:8-9; see also Climate, Weather

Seattle (Washington) vol.9:22; vol.12:23

Seaweed vol.10:13

Seed vol.4:41; vol.9:13; vol.10:19; vol.11:41; see also Crop, Plant

Semaphore vol.4:36

Seminole people vol.8:32

Senate vol.4:26; vol.6:43

Serbia and Montenegro vol.10:20; vol.12:41; see also Europe

Shakespeare, William vol.3:47

Shark vol.10:21; see also Fish

Sharp, Cecil vol.4:43

Shawnee people vol.5:47

Sheep vol.1:35; vol.2:46; vol.4:14; vol.9:7; vol.10:22, 31; vol.11:29, 48; vol.12:22, 45; see also Mammal

Shellfish vol.7:38

Shepard, Alan vol.10:46

Sherpa people vol.8:11

Ship vol.4:22; vol.5:16; vol.8:44; vol.9:22; vol.10:23; vol.12:17, 23, 29; see also Barge, Port, Transportation, Waterway

Shofar vol.12:34

Shona people vol.12:48

Shoshone people vol.10:6

Shrew vol.7:19

Shrimp vol.3:30; vol.4:37

Sign language vol.6:38

Sikhism vol.5:46; vol.10:24

Silk vol.2:48; vol.11:22

Silver vol.7:34; vol.8:13, 46; vol.9:43

Singapore vol.10:25; see also Asia, Port

Sioux people vol.7:41; vol.8:23; vol.10:26, 43

Sitar vol.8:6

Sitting Bull vol.10:26

Skeleton vol.10:27; vol.12:15; see also Human Body, Vertebrate

Skiing vol.2:24; vol.8:4, 26; vol.11:21; vol.12:14

Skunk vol.10:28; see also Mammal

Skyscraper vol.5:43

Slavery vol.3:5; vol.7:7, 36; vol.10:29; vol.11:45; vol.12:13; Index:16; see also Civil War; Lincoln, Abraham; Tubman, Harriet

Sleeping Sickness vol.4:42

Slovakia vol.10:30; see also Czech Republic, Europe

Slovenia vol.10:20, 31; see also Serbia and Montenegro

Slug vol.6:7; vol.7:38; vol.10:32; see also Mollusk, Snail

Smell vol.10:33; vol.11:24; see also Taste, Touch

Smithsonian Institution vol.12:24

Snail vol.6:7; vol.7:38; vol.10:34; see also Mollusk, Slug

Snake vol.1:34; vol.3:41; vol.5:28; vol.9:37; vol.10:7, 35; see also Reptile

Snake River vol.5:42

Snow White vol.4:29

Snowboarding vol.8:4

Soccer vol.4:23, 25

Soil vol.9:9, 48; vol.10:36; vol.12:12, 20; see also Crop, Farming

Solar system vol.9:12; vol.10:37; vol.11:7, 18; see also Space Exploration, Spacecraft

Solomon Islands vol.1:36

Somalia vol.10:38; see also Africa

Sorghum vol.8:10; vol.11:17

Sound vol.4:6, 21; vol.7:6; vol.8:7, 36; vol.10:39; see also Ear

South Africa vol.1:8; vol.2:4, 18; vol.4:7; vol.10:40; Index:8, 15; see also Africa

South America vol.3:21; vol.10:41; vol.12:29; Index:4; *see also* Continent

South Carolina vol.10:42; *see also* United States of America

South Dakota vol.10:43; *see also* United States of America

South Korea vol.8:24; vol.10:44; *see also* Asia, North Korea

South Pole vol.1:22; vol.7:16

Soviet Union vol.10:4

Soybean vol.1:31; vol.2:31

Space vol.3:16; vol.10:45, 46; vol.11:7

Space exploration vol.1:32; vol.6:28; vol.9:12, 42; vol.10:45; Index:15, 17; *see also* Moon, Planet, Spacecraft

Spacecraft vol.10:46; *see also* Moon, Space Exploration

Spain vol.10:47; vol.11:29; *see also* Europe

Spanish mission vol.8:16

Spanish-American war vol.9:47

Spice vol.10:38

Spider vol.10:48; *see also* Invertebrate

Spore vol.4:31; vol.5:7; vol.9:13

Sport vol.2:35; vol.6:11, 37; vol.8:4, 13, 33; vol.10:9; vol.12:27, 31

Squid vol.7:38; vol.11:4; *see also* Mollusk, Sea Life

Squirrel vol.5:28; vol.11:5; *see also* Mammal

Sri Lanka vol.11:6, 41; *see also* Asia

Stanton, Elizabeth Cady vol.1:25

Star vol.11:7, 18; *see also* Solar System, Sun

Star Wars vol.9:42

Star-Spangled Banner vol.1:17; vol.11:8; Index:16; *see also* American Flag, Flag

Starfish vol.11:9; *see also* Invertebrate, Sea Life

Statue vol.5:30; vol.10:10

Statue of Liberty vol.9:22; vol.11:10; Index:17; *see also* New York

Steam engine vol.4:22; vol.9:32; vol.11:39, 44

Steel vol.6:12; vol.7:16, 27; vol.10:23; vol.12:22

Stegosaurus vol.11:11; *see also* Dinosaur, Fossil

Stem vol.9:13; vol.11:12; *see also* Plant

Stone vol.2:21; vol.11:13

Stone Age vol.11:13; *see also* Bronze Age, Iron Age

Stonehenge Index:12

Story vol.6:42; vol.7:9; vol.8:8, 34; vol.9:27; vol.11:14; vol.12:17; *see also* Fable, Fairy Tale, Legend, Literature, Myth

Straits of Mackinac vol.7:31

Stringed Instrument vol.4:32; vol.8:6, 7, 36; vol.11:15; *see also* Music, Musical Instrument, Orchestra

Submarine vol.1:28; vol.11:16; *see also* Ship, Transportation

Sudan vol.1:8; vol.11:17; Index:4; *see also* Africa

Suez Canal vol.4:14; vol.12:29

Sugar cane vol.1:47; vol.2:11; vol.3:11, 31, 45; vol.5:20; vol.6:18; vol.7:11, 36; vol.9:7, 8, 26; vol.11:43

Sumer vol.7:9; Index:12

Sun vol.3:34; vol.4:7; vol.7:5, 42; vol.10:37; vol.11:7, 18; vol.12:28, 30; Index:8-9; *see also* Solar System, Star

Sunflower vol.4:41; vol.12:7

Supreme Court vol.6:25

Swallow vol.7:33

Swan vol.10:16; vol.11:19; *see also* Bird

Swan, Thomas vol.4:17

Swan Lake vol.1:43

Sweden vol.6:4; vol.11:20; vol.12:17; Index:8; *see also* Europe

Switzerland vol.11:21; *see also* Europe

Syria vol.11:22; *see also* Asia

T

Tadpole vol.5:5; vol.11:34

Tae kwon do vol.10:44

Taiwan vol.11:23; *see also* Asia, China

Tasmania vol.1:36

Taste vol.11:24; *see also* Smell, Touch

Tchaikovsky, Peter Ilich vol.1:43

Tea vol.1:34; vol.6:19, 30, 40; vol.10:5; vol.11:6, 23; vol.12:6

Tea ceremony vol.6:19

Telegraph vol.3:17; vol.4:11

Telephone vol.3:17; vol.4:11; vol.6:39; vol.9:31; vol.11:25; *see also* Communication

Telescope vol.5:22; vol.10:45; vol.11:18

Television vol.2:33; vol.3:13, 17, 47; vol.4:17; vol.6:39; vol.7:9, 16; vol.9:31; vol.11:26; Index:14; *see also* Communication, Radio

Temperature vol.1:22, 28; vol.6:47; vol.7:24; vol.8:21; vol.11:18; vol.12:30; Index:8-9

Tennessee vol.11:27; *see also* United States of America

Tenochtitlan vol.7:30

Termite vol.11:28; *see also* Insect

Terrorism vol.2:26

Texas vol.2:26; vol.11:29; *see also* Bush, George W.; United States of America

Textiles vol.2:31; vol.8:22, 43; vol.9:39; vol.10:20, 42; vol.11:22, 29, 47, 48

Thailand vol.11:30; *see also* Asia

Thames Barrier vol.4:39

Thames River vol.12:8

Thanksgiving vol.5:32; Index:16

Theater vol.3:47; vol.7:9; vol.11:31; *see also* Drama, Opera

Theodore Roosevelt National Park vol.8:23

Thunder vol.7:6

Tiger vol.1:34; vol.2:38; vol.11:32; vol.12:16; *see also* Cat, Mammal

Tigris River vol.6:10

Time vol.2:29; vol.3:34; vol.11:33; *see also* Calendar, Measurement, Season

Tin vol.7:27

Titanic Index:14

Toad vol.5:28; vol.11:34; *see also* Amphibian, Frog, Metamorphosis

Toadstool see Fungus

Tobacco vol.2:34; vol.3:27; vol.8:22; vol.10:42; vol.11:27; vol.12:18, 48

Tokyo vol.6:19

Tomato vol.3:29

Tongue vol.11:24

Tooth vol.11:35; *see also* Human Body

Torah vol.6:24

Tornado vol.7:37; vol.8:10; vol.11:36; vol.12:30; *see also* Hurricane, Weather

Tortoise vol.9:37; vol.11:37; *see also* Reptile, Turtle

Touch vol.11:38; *see also* Smell, Taste

Tragedy vol.3:47

Train vol.9:32; vol.11:39, 40; *see also* Railroad, Transportation

Transportation vol.1:10; vol.2:12, 25, 35, 36; vol.5:35, 36; vol.7:48; vol.9:32, 41; vol.10:23; vol.11:39, 40, 44; vol.12:29, 31; *see also* Railroad, Road, Waterway

Treaty of Paris vol.1:18

Treaty of Versailles vol.12:41

Tree vol.2:30; vol.4:45; vol.6:40; vol.9:33; vol.10:18; vol.11:41; vol.12:38; *see also* Forest, Rain Forest, Wood

Triceratops vol.11:42; vol.12:15; *see also* Dinosaur, Fossil

Trinidad and Tobago vol.11:43; *see also* South America

Tropics vol.3:7; vol.9:33; vol.10:18

Truck vol.11:44; *see also* Road, Transportation

Trumpet vol.8:6; vol.12:34

Tuareg people vol.6:47

Tuatara vol.9:37

Tuba vol.12:34

Tubman, Harriet vol.11:45

Tulip vol.8:12; vol.11:12

Tundra vol.1:28; vol.11:46; *see also* Arctic

Tunisia vol.11:47; *see also* Africa
Turkey vol.11:48; vol.12:41; *see also* Asia, Europe
Turtle vol.4:13; vol.5:8; vol.9:37; vol.12:4; *see also* Reptile, Tortoise
Tutankhamen vol.7:27
Tutsi people vol.9:6; vol.10:5
Twin Towers Index:17
Typhoon vol.5:40
Tyrannosaurus vol.3:42; vol.11:42; vol.12:5; *see also* Dinosaur, Fossil

Uganda vol.12:6; *see also* Africa
Ukraine vol.12:7; *see also* Europe
Ultrasound vol.10:39
Underground Railroad vol.11:45
United Kingdom vol.4:23; vol.8:25; vol.10:9; vol.12:8, 41, 42; *see also* Europe
United Nations vol.12:9, 33; *see also* Wilson, Woodrow
United States of America (U.S.A.) vol.1:18, 42; vol.3:20, 35; vol.4:26; vol.11:10, 29; vol.12:10, 24, 25, 42; Index:4, 9, 18-9, 20-21, 23-25; *see also* Native Americans, North America
Ural Mountains vol.4:25; vol.10:4
U.S. Space and Rocket Center vol.1:11
Utah vol.6:37; vol.12:11; *see also* United States of America

V

Valley vol.12:12; *see also* Mountain, River
Van Gogh, Vincent vol.1:33; vol.8:12
Vanessa-Mae vol.11:15
Vanilla vol.7:15
Vatican City vol.6:16
Venezuela vol.12:13; *see also* South America
Venice (Italy) vol.6:16
Vermont vol.7:23; vol.12:14; *see also* United States of America
Vertebrate vol.12:15; *see also* Invertebrate, Skeleton
Veterans Day vol.5:32
Victoria Falls vol.12:46;
Vietnam vol.12:16; *see also* Asia
Vietnam War Index:17
Vikings vol.8:8, 26; vol.12:17; *see also* Denmark, Norway, Sweden
Vinson Massif vol.1:22
Violin vol.11:15
Virginia vol.1:18; vol.3:12; vol.6:21; vol.12:18, 25, 31; *see also* American Revolution, Colonial America, United States of America

Virus vol.12:19; *see also* Bacteria
Volcano vol.1:29; vol.3:23; vol.4:7; vol.5:18, 22, 41, 48; vol.6:14, 16, 19; vol.8:4, 19, 29; vol.9:7, 43; vol.12:20, 23; *see also* Mountain
Vulture vol.12:21; *see also* Bird

Wagner, Richard vol.8:34
Wales vol.12:8, 22; *see also* Europe, United Kingdom
Walrus vol.1:28
War of 1812 vol.11:9
Washington vol.9:33; vol.12:23; *see also* Rain Forest, United States of America
Washington, D.C. vol.5:45; vol.6:31, 43; vol.7:22; vol.12:24; Index:18; *see also* Executive Branch, Government, Judicial Branch, Legislative Branch
Washington, George vol.1:18; vol.5:32; vol.12:25; Index:16; *see also* American Revolution
Wasp vol.12:26; *see also* Bee, Insect
Water vol.5:37; vol.6:35, 47; vol.7:24; vol.8:4, 10, 12, 14; vol.9:40; vol.11:40, 41; vol.12:12, 20, 27, 28; *see also* Water Cycle
Water Cycle vol.12:28; *see also* Water
Waterfall vol.10:41; vol.12:12, 46
Waterway vol.1:48; vol.12:29; *see also* Barge, Ship, Transportation
Weather vol.3:7; vol.4:7; vol.5:40, 41; vol.10:18; vol.11:36; vol.12:30; Index:8-9; *see also* Climate
Wedge vol.7:14
West Virginia vol.12:31; *see also* United States of America
Whale vol.1:22; vol.7:19; vol.12:15, 32; *see also* Dolphin, Mammal
Wheat vol.1:34; vol.3:29; vol.8:10, 23, 37, 43; vol.9:44; vol.10:4, 7, 19, 30, 47; vol.12:23
Wheel vol.7:14; vol.11:40
Wheelbarrow vol.2:48
White House vol.12:24
Wildebeest vol.4:44; vol.7:8
Wilson, Woodrow vol.11:9; vol.12:33; *see also* Star-Spangled Banner
Wind farm vol.4:17
Wind instrument vol.8:36; vol.12:34; *see also* Music, Musical Instrument
Windmill vol.5:22; vol.8:12
Wisconsin vol.12:35; *see also* United States of America
Wolf vol.1:12, 34; vol.3:24, 43; vol.4:25; vol.8:21; vol.12:36, 45; *see also* Dog, Mammal

Wolverine vol.12:37; *see also* Mammal
Women's rights vol.1:25; vol.11:45; Index:17
Wood vol.11:41; vol.12:38; *see also* Forest, Rain Forest, Tree
Woodlouse vol.3:30; vol.12:39; *see also* Crustacean, Invertebrate
Woodpecker vol.12:40; *see also* Bird
Wool vol.1:35; vol.10:22
World Health Organization vol.12:9
World War I vol.8:33; vol.12:33, 41, 42; Index:14; *see also* Wilson, Woodrow; World War II
World War II vol.6:24, 28; vol.7:31; vol.8:33; vol.9:46; vol.12:42; Index:14, 17; *see also* Roosevelt, Franklin D.
World Wide Web vol.6:6
Worm vol.6:7; vol.10:36; vol.12:43; *see also* Invertebrate
Wright brothers vol.1:10; vol.8:22; vol.12:44; Index:14, 17; *see also* Airplane
Wyoming vol.10:6; vol.12:45; *see also* United States of America

Yale University vol.3:8, 19
Yeast *see* Fungus
Yellowstone National Park vol.12:45
Yom Kippur vol.12:34
Yugoslavia vol.10:20

Z

Zambezi River vol.12:46;
Zambia vol.12:46; *see also* Africa
Zebra vol.7:8; vol.12:47; *see also* Horse, Mammal
Zimbabwe vol.12:48; Index:13; *see also* Africa
Zoologist vol.1:20
Zworykin, Vladimir vol.11:26